Giovanna Magi

Paris

A COMPLETE GUIDE FOR VISITING THE CITY

12 ITINERARIES
140 COLOUR ILLUSTRATIONS
MAP OF THE CITY
MAP OF THE MÉTRO
VERSAILLES

ⅢB BONECHI

INDEX OF THE ITINERARIES

◄ **A suggestive view of the Pyramid of the Louvre.**

Night view of the celebrated Eiffel Tower.

Welcome to Paris

"Ladies and gentlemen, please fasten your seat belts and extinguish all cigarettes: we are beginning our descent and within ten minutes we will be landing at the Charles de Gaulle airport." Perhaps your heart beat a little faster when the hostess made this announcement, because it meant you were arriving in Paris for the first time, with a feeling of excitement about what might lie ahead. At the airport (either Orly or Roissy-Charles de Gaulle) you took the bus which has left you at the Invalides or the Porte Maillot terminal. Here you have to decide how to get to your hotel: by taxi or on Paris's underground railway, the Métro?

THE MÉTRO

You begin at once to behave like a Parisian and take the Métro. For your ticket, buy a carnet'' (10 tickets = 10 trips) because it is cheaper. You will use them all because wherever you go the Métro is the fastest and least expensive way to travel. Large maps, both outside and inside the stations, show all the Métro lines in different colours. The map of the Métro in this guide will also help you learn how to travel on the system. To work out which line you have to take, look at the station at the end of the line on which your station is located.

The directions are very clearly shown on indicator boards above each platform. And the names of the stations along the various lines are shown on the large blue and white signs in the corridors. You will also find them in the carriages. And there will always be some kind person prepared to help you.

Once in the carriage, of course, you will become absorbed in watching your fellow travellers. Paris, like every other great city, has its typical figures. Men sitting with their noses in the newspaper, women reading novels or busy knitting — almost all of them have to make a long journey to reach the place where they work. And of course there are the usual couples of lovers involved with each other and totally oblivious of those around them.

STAYING IN PARIS

Once you have freshened up in your hotel room after your long and tiring trip, you will probably decide, full of enthusiasm and curiosity, to begin without delay your personal conquest of Paris, about which you have heard so much. And there are many things to see in this enormous and complex city. There is the city of the working people, the ones you meet in the crowded Métro in the evening rush hours with their tired faces; the same ones you see at eight o'clock in the morning or at midday as they sip a "petit blanc sec" (glass of white wine) or a "café arrosé" (coffee with a dash of cognac added), standing "au zinc" (at the counter) of the bar on the corner.

Then there is the city of high fashion, with its boutiques full of splendid clothes around Place Vendôme, Faubourg St-Honoré or Rue de la Paix.

There is the picturesque city, the city of the artists and intellectuals: in the "villages" of St-Germain-des-Prés or Montmartre, or along the Seine embankments with their "bouquinistes" (the sellers of second-hand books and old prints). And there is the historical city, with its monuments, testifying to its long and fascinating history.

You will certainly want to sit outside in an open-air café and enjoy a "grand crème" (milk coffee) with a "croissant", a snack to keep you going until lunchtime. There will be no lack of company there, because the Parisians spend a great deal of time in the bars and cafés at all hours of the day and night, chatting, talking of politics or business — talking of anything and everything. The typical Parisian is a great talker and is often mocking and ironic. Gesticulating, he discusses the day's events in a colourful language, full of Parisian slang or "argot", with the flat, rapid Parisian accent. The cabdrivers and the "quatre-saisons" vendors (the ones who sell fruit and vegetables from their barrows) are famous for their salty, colourful language.

SHOPPING

You will probably also want to begin at once doing some shopping, even before you go looking for special souvenirs. Shopping in Paris will give you an idea of the vitality of the city, whether you are buying food or any other article. It is a large city where the people work hard. Shops selling food are open from 8.30 a.m. (the bakeries from 7) to 1 p.m. and from 4 p.m. to 7.30 p.m. Other shops (fashion boutiques, bookshops, hairdressers, etc.) are mostly open from 9 a.m. to 7 p.m. without interruption. Food shops are also open on Sunday morning, but on Monday most of them are closed (some only in the morning).

Remember that in many shops (fashion shops, those selling perfume, jewellery or other luxury goods), if you show your passport and a special card issued by your bank or by American Express, you can make a saving on sales tax. There is no embarkation tax at the Paris airports.

FRENCH CUISINE

And now a word about Frenche cuisine... First of all we should mention that you can have a light meal at any hour of the day: in the "Brasseries" especially you can have an "assiette anglaise" (cold meat and ham), a "croque-monsieur" (toasted ham and cheese sandwich), or sandwiches of any kind. If you feel so inclined or do not have time to sit down, you can buy various things to eat as you are walking: hot dogs, crêpes (pancakes), wafers or "krapfens" (doughnuts). These can be bought at stands in many of the outside cafés, especially around St-Michel and the Odéon. But for a more "serious" meal, there are the real restaurants. Obviously you will not find caviar and pâte de foie gras in all the restaurants. But there are dishes you will find on almost every menu, the typically French dishes, many of which come from the provinces where they originated and have been adopted by the Parisians. "There is no greater gourmet than Paris..." Of course "steak pommes frite" (steak and potato chips) does not need to be described, though we should mention that the Parisians usually eat it "à point" (rare only in the middle) or often "bleu", meaning well cooked on the outside and almost raw in the middle. Then there is "Pot-au-feu", boiled beef served with vegetables (leeks, carrots, rape and celery) which have been boiled in the meat broth. "Boeuf bourguignon" is beef cut up in small pieces and cooked on a slow fire in a thick, highly flavoured sauce, with red wine, mushrooms and pieces of bacon. "Hachis Parmentier" is a dish made from potatoes cooked in the oven with a meat filling. "Haricot de mouton" is mutton cut into small pieces, cooked for a long time in a thick, tasty sauce, in which white beans are cooked at the same time.

7

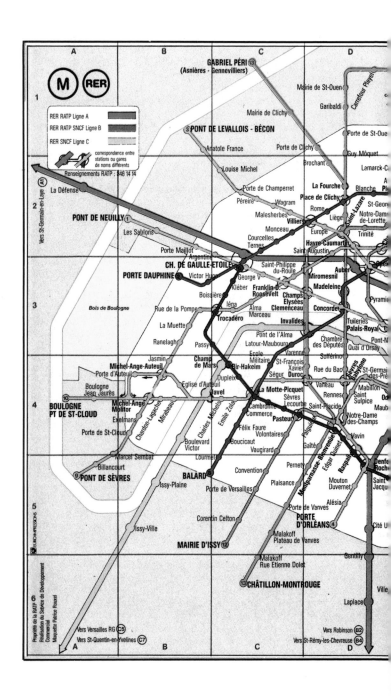

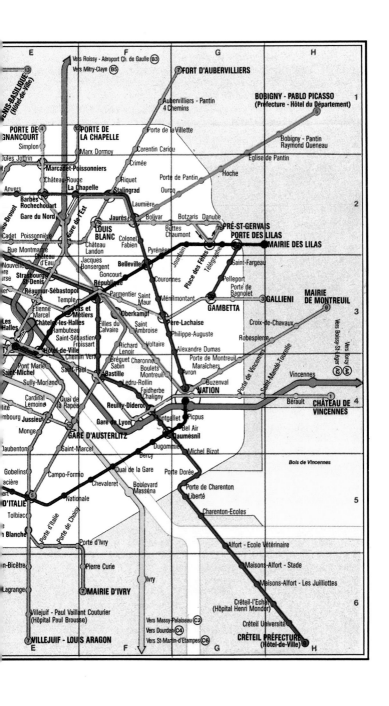

By adding lard and sausage with garlic, plus a tomato sauce, to this mutton, we have the highly flavoursome "Cassoulet toulousain". "Epaule de mouton" is a shoulder of mutton from which the bone has been removed and replaced with stuffing; it is served with potatoes and rape cooked in the same sauce. "Blanquette de veau" is veal cooked in white sauce with white wine and mushrooms, served with boiled potatoes or rice. "Boudin pommes en l'air" is black pudding or blood fritter, roasted and served with a thick, non-sweetened and slightly tart apple sauce. "Quenelles" are balls made from bread, eggs, meat or fish and served with various types of sauces: a light, delicate dish. "Bouchées à la Reine" (or small "Vol-au-vent") consist of a pastry crust with veal sweetbreads and brains in Bechamel and are greatly appreciated by the connoisseurs. Among desserts we might mention "Œufs à la neige" (also called "Floating Islands"), large balls of egg white beaten to a thick consistency, soaked in milk and served with vanilla custard. "Nègre en chemise" is made from chocolate, eggs and butter, served with whipped cream. "Crêpes" are pancakes, served hot with sugar, jam, or rum, Maraschino or Gran Marnier flambé. The cheeses, one of the triumphs of French gastronomy, should not be forgotten. As for seafood (oysters, clams, prawns, sea urchins, coquilles Saint-Jacques), snails and frogs' legs, these cannot be explained: you have to try them yourself...

TOUR OF THE CITY

Now for your tour of the city: there are, of course, tours organised by agencies (especially in the Opéra area), which can give you a rapid panoramic idea of Paris. But we hope you will have time to go on foot and really see the city. Nevertheless you will certainly enjoy a cruise along the Seine in a "Bateau-Mouche", which offers a view of Paris from an unusual angle. During the cruise you can also have lunch or dinner (cruises leave from Pont de l'Alma, Quai de Montebello and the Square du Vert-Galant at the Pont Neuf).
To complete this panorama aimed at helping you in your early stages, a few words on "Paris by night". So much has been said about it... We should remind you, by the way, that you can find all the programmes and times of the cinemas, theatres, concerts, lectures, and other performances such as "sound and light" shows and exhibitions in two small specialised magazines — "Pariscope" and the "Officile des Spectacles" — which come out once a week, on Wednesdays. If you understand French really well and are interested in current events and politics, you will enjoy the "Chansonniers" (Caveau de la République, Théâtre de Dix-Heures, the Deux-Anes); if you are a lover of songs and variety shows, you will be interested in the Olympia, the Bobino and the "cafés-théâtres".

Some cabarets have dinner with a show and dinner with dancing, and here the choice is great, ranging from singers to strip-tease.

Finally there are the famous "boîtes de nuit" — the night clubs around Place Pigalle and Place Blanche and on the hill of Montmartre: there is an endless succession of them, with their brightly lit signs designed to excite the curiosity of the passer-by. Here the whole strange world of Paris's night life can be seen. Montparnasse, Saint-Germain-des-Prés and the Champs-Élysées offer yet more amusement by night. You can dance to the rhythm of their typical bands or be entranced by the music of the Gipsy violins.

We should only remind you of what is true of amusement places all over the world: mind your wallet, sir, and don't leave your purse at your table, madam. Don't be too trusting when you meet a pleasant face. And remember, champagne is bubbly but it can go to your head — and make anybody you meet all too likable!

With these wise words of advice, we can only leave you to go out and get to know Paris, the city which always takes great pleasure in welcoming friends who have come from afar.

Micheline Gille

The numerous boats which take tourists along the Seine.

Flower Stalls near Notre-Dame.

Brief history of the city

Paris was probably founded by the Gauls, who built a small settlement on the left bank of the Seine. The city is mentioned, with the name of Lutetia, by Julius Caesar who came here in 53 B.C.

As a result of the continual menace of the barbarian invasions, this original settlement was moved to the Île-de-la-Cité, and from there it expanded along the banks of the river. The residence first of the Merovingian and then of the Carolingian kings, Paris became a real capital in 987, when Hugo, the first Capetian king, founded a new and powerful dynasty. One of Paris' moments of maximum splendour was between 1180 and 1223, when Philippe Auguste came to the throne: the construction of the Louvre was begun and the University was founded. During the reign of St Louis IX, the Sainte-Chapelle was built and work on Notre-Dame was continued. But the next dynasty, that of the Valois kings, brought wars and catastrophe, disorder and civil discord to Paris. Although Charles V briefly restored order, the fighting between the Armagnacs and Burgundians became more and more savage: this led to the occupation of France by England, and in 1430 Henry VI was crowned king of France.

In 1437 Charles VII reconquered Paris, but the population was exhausted by the bloody revolts alternating with epidemics of the plague. Although throughout the 16th century the kings preferred to live in the castles of the Loire rather than in the capital, this did not end the internecine struggles in Paris itself. The spread of the Protestant religion created struggles which for a long time rent Paris and the whole of France, culminating in the massacre of the Huguenots on the infamous night of St Bartholomew (24 August 1572). After Henri III had been assassinated in 1589, the city was besieged for four long years until finally it opened its gates to Henri IV, who had converted to Catholicism.

At the beginning of the 17th century, however, Paris already had no less than 30,000 inhabitants. The city became more and more important under the powerful Cardinal Richelieu and during the new dynasty of the Bourbon kings: at the time of Louis XIV, the Sun King, it had half a million inhabitants. But Paris earned its real place in history after 1789, the year of the French Revolution, which was to mark the birth of the modern world. The long years of terror, in which many human lives were lost and irreparable damage done to so many works of art, were forgotten in the splendour of the Empire and the dazzling court created by Napoleon, crowned Emperor in 1804.

From 1804 to 1814 Paris was constantly being enriched: the

Arch of Triumph was built, the Vendôme column erected and the Louvre enlarged. After the fall of other monarchies, those of Charles X and Louis-Philippe Bourbon-Orléans, the Second Republic was born and then Napoleon III took the throne. He entrusted the task of replanning the city to Baron Haussmann: the markets of Les Halles were built, the Bois de Vincennes and Bois de Boulogne laid out, the Opéra erected, and the great boulevards, typical expression of this historical era, were opened up.

The year 1871 marked a new and sad page in the history of Paris with the Commune (18 March-28 May). Many splendid historic buildings were lost in these days of rebellion and destruction by fire: among others, the Hôtel de Ville and the palace of the Tuileries. But Paris had new moments of splendour at the beginning of this century, with the World Exhibitions, the construction of the Grand Palais and the Petit Palais, and the birth of important movements of art, painting and literature. Unfortunately the city had yet to suffer the bombardments and destruction of two long wars. During the second world war it fell into the hands of the German Army in 1940 and was not liberated by the Allies until 1944. But from that moment until today, as a city finally alive and free, Paris has resumed its place in the history of culture and humanity.

The Beaubourg seen from rue St Martin.

Right side of Notre-Dame seen from the Montebello Quay.

NOTRE-DAME – **Façade**

THE CITÉ *(Métro: line 4 – Cité station).*

Pont Neuf – Square du Vert Galant – Place du Parvis – **Notre-Dame** – **Palais de Justice** – **Sainte-Chapelle** – **Conciergerie** – **Ile St-Louis**.

Pont Neuf.

THE CITÉ

The Cité, centre of the city's life since the 3rd century, was founded here on what was the largest of the islands in the Seine. It was the first settlement and first religious centre, and here were erected the Cathedral and the Palais de Justice. Numerous bridges link it to the banks of the Seine, along which run the picturesque "quais". One of the most animated and colourful of the quays is the **Quai de Montebello,** extending between the bridges called Pont de l'Archevêché and Pont au Double: it is full of life and its parapets are lined with the typical "bouquinistes", the sellers of rare and strange books and prints old and new.

Lean arches of Pont Neuf.

PONT NEUF AND SQUARE DU VERT GALANT — Walking along the Quai St Michel and the Quai des Grands Augustins, we reach this bridge, which is the oldest in Paris, planned by Du Cerceau and Des Illes: begun in 1578 under Henri III and completed under Henri IV in 1606, it has two slender round arches and in the middle of it is the **equestrian statue of Henri IV**. The square is reached by a stairway behind the statue of the king. It is the furthermost point of the Cité and one of the most beautiful parts of Paris.

PLACE DU PARVIS — Turning back along the celebrated Quai des Orfèvres, we pass the headquarters of the Judicial Police at number 36 before reaching the Place du Parvis, which is the point from which road distances in France are measured: the bronze plaque in the centre of the square in front of the cathedral indicates the starting point for all the nation's roads. On the north side of the square stands the grandiose **Hôtel-Dieu,** a hospice founded in the 7th century but rebuilt between 1868 and 1878; on the west side is the **headquarters of the Préfecture de Police.** Overlooking the square is the imposing Notre-Dame, the cathedral of Paris.

Equestrian statue of Henri IV.

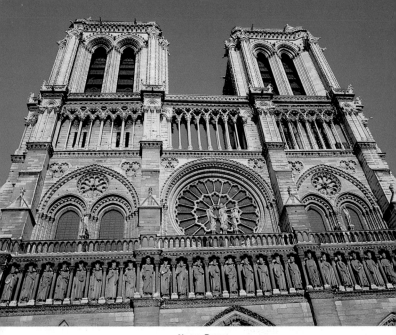

Notre-Dame.

NOTRE-DAME

The cathedral of Notre-Dame stands on the site of a Christian basilica which had in turn been built on the site of a temple from the Roman era. Its construction was begun in 1163, under Bishop Maurice de Sully: first the chancel was built, followed over the years by the nave and aisles and the façade, completed by Bishop Eudes de Sully in about 1200, the towers being finished in 1245. The architects Jean de Chelles and Pierre de Montreuil then constructed the chapels in the aisles and in the chancel. Towards 1250 the façade of th north arm of the transept was also completed; the other, that of the south arm, was not begun until eight years later. The church could be said to be completed in 1345. In 1793 it ran the risk of being demolished; at this time, during the French Revolution, it was dedicated to the Goddess of Reason. Reconsecrated in 1802, it was the scene two years later of the coronation of Napoleon I by Pope Pius VII. It was restored by Viollet-le-Duc between 1844 and 1864.

THE FAÇADE — It is divided vertically into three parts by pilasters and horizontally into three areas by its two galleries; in the lowest zone are the three portals. Above the portals runs the **Gallery of the Kings,** with its 28 statues representing the kings of Israel and Judea. In 1793 the people, seeing them as the hated French kings, knocked them down, but they were later put back in place. The central zone of the façade contains two great mullioned windows, on either side of a rose window measuring more than 30 feet in diameter (1220-1225). In the centre are the *statues of the Virgin and Child with angels,* on either side *Adam and Eve.* Above this part is a gallery of tightly carved arches which link the two towers at the sides; though never completed, the towers contain splendid, extremely high two-light windows. Viollet-le-Duc filled this uppermost zone with gargoyles, grotesque figures with strange and fantastic forms, projecting from pinnacles, spires and extensions of the walls.

Central portal. On this is depicted the Last Judgment: on the pier which divides it in two is the *statue of Christ,* while in the embrasures there are panels with the *personifications of the vices and virtues and statues of the apostles.* Around the curve of the arch are the *Heavenly Court, Paradise* and *Hell.* The lunette containing the *Last Judgment* is divided into three parts, dominated by the figure of Christ, flanked by the Virgin, St John and angels with symbols of the Passion. Below are the Blessed on one side and the Damned on the other. In the lower part, the *Resurrection.*

Right portal. Also called the Portal of St Anne, it dates from 1160-1170, with reliefs from the 12th and 13th centuries. On the dividing pier, a *statue of St Marcel.* In the lunette, the *Virgin between two angels* and at the sides *Bishop Maurice de Sully* and *King Louis XII.*

Left portal. Also called the Portal of the Virgin, it is the finest of the three. On the dividing pier, the *Virgin and Child,* a modern work. In the lunette above, the *Death, Glorification*

NOTRE-DAME — **Portals.**

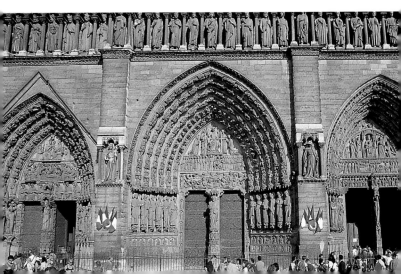

NOTRE-DAME – **The apse lit up.**

and Assumption of the Virgin. On the door-posts are depicted the *Months of the year,* in the embrasures figures of saints and angels.

RIGHT SIDE – On this side of the church is the *Portal of St Stephen,* begun by Jean de Chelles in 1258 and completed by Pierre de Montreuil, with its splendid large rose window and another smaller one in the cusp. Here can be seen the **spire,** soaring above the centre of the cathedral 295 feet high: it was rebuilt by Viollet-le-Duc, who depicted himself among the Apostles and Evangelists which decorate it.

INTERIOR – Its dimensions are impressive: 427 feet long, 164 feet wide and 115 feet high, it can contain no less than 9000 persons. The interior is divided into nave and four aisles by cylindrical piers 16 feet in diameter, with a double ambulatory around the transept and chancel. The **rose window** in the façade, above the 18th-century organ, depicts the Signs of the Zodiac, the Months and the Vices and Virtues. Above the arcades runs a gallery with double openings, surmounted in turn by ample windows. The **chapels** following one after the other up to the transept have a wealth of works of art from the 17th and 18th centuries: outstanding are two paintings by Le Brun, the *Martyrdom of St Stephen* and the *Martyrdom of St Andrew,* in the first and second chapels on the right respectively. The two ends of the transept have splendid stained-glass windows from the 13th century. The one in the north transept (about 1250) depicts subjects from the Old Testament with the *Virgin and Child* in the

NOTRE-DAME – The rose window at the south head of the transept
and the inside of the cathedral.

centre; the one in the south transept, restored in the 18th century, represents *Christ in the act of blessing* in the centre, surrounded by Apostles and Martyrs, with the Wise and Foolish Virgins. After the transept comes the **chancel**: on the pier to the right as one enters is the celebrated *statue of Notre-Dame-de-Paris* (Our Lady of Paris), a 14th-century work once in the St-Aignan Chapel. Around the chancel are carved wooden choir stalls (18th century); on the high altar, a *statue of the Pietà,* by Nicolas Coustou, in the centre, with *Louis XIII,* by Guillaume Coustou, and *Louis XIV,* by Coysevox, at the sides. An uncompleted marble chancel screen, decorated with reliefs (works by Jean Ravy and Jean le Bouteiller), separates the chancel from the ambulatory, and in the radial chapels around it are numerous tombs. On the right, between the Chapelle St-Denis and the Chapelle St-Madeleine, is the entrance to the **Treasury**: it contains much sacred silverware and important relics, among them a fragment of the True Cross, the Crown of Thorns and the Holy Nail.

APSE — This is one of the most daring apses of the Middle Ages, with flying buttresses 50 feet long, built by Jean Ravy (14th century).

Next to the apse of Notre-Dame is the **Square Jean XXIII**: its present appearance and its Neo-Gothic fountain date from a reorganisation project in 1844. We now walk along the **Quai aux Fleurs** and **Quai de Corse**, where there is a picturesque and typical flower market every day, substituted on Sundays by an equally colourful bird market. Beyond the **Bridge of Notre-Dame,** we reach the headquarters of the **Tribunal de Commerce** and then the bridge called the **Pont au Change,** the name of which derives from the many moneychangers' shops concentrated here in the Middle Ages.

PALAIS DE JUSTICE

This is a huge complex of buildings, including the **Palais de Justice** itself, the **Sainte-Chapelle** and the **Conciergerie.** On this same site the Roman rulers had their administrative and military headquarters; the kings of the Merovingian dynasty followed their example, and later the Capetians erected a chapel and a keep here. In the 13th century, St Louis IX built the Sainte-Chapelle and in the following century Philippe the Fair had the Conciergerie palace constructed. In 1358, after the bloody revolts of the Parisians headed by Etienne Marcel, Charles V decided to move his residence to the Louvre and leave the palace here to the Parliament which used it to house the supreme court of justice of the kingdom. In later times, the buildings were repeatedly damaged by fires: in 1618 the Grande Salle was burnt, in 1630 the tall spire of the Sainte-Chapelle, in 1737 the Debtors' Court and in 1776 the Marchande Gallery. The judicial system, which until then had remained intact, was overturned by the Revolution. The new courts were established in the old building, which was given the name of Palais de Justice (Palace of Justice). Important works of restoration carried out under the direction of Viollet-le-Duc gave the building its present-day appearance. Facing Boulevard du Palais is its monumental façade. On the right, the **Tour de l'Horloge,** or Clock Tower, dating from the 14th century. The clock dates from 1334, while the reliefs are by Germain Pilon (1585). After this comes the façade of the Civil Court, 14th-century in style though it was built in 1853. In the centre of the façade, a high wrought-iron gateway (1783-1785) leads into the **May Courtyard,** built in 1786 by Antoine and Desmaisons. From here, through a vaulted passageway on the left, one reaches the Sainte-Chapelle.

SAINTE-CHAPELLE

Built for St Louis IX to contain the Crown of Thorns which the sovereign had bought in 1239 in Venice, it was designed by Pierre de Montreuil, consisting of two chapels, one above the other, which were consecrated in 1248. Above its high base (which corresponds to the lower chapel), there are

Sainte-Chapelle.

SAINTE-CHAPELLE– The lower church and, on the right, the upper one with its famous stained glass windows.

vast windows crowned with cusps. The steep sloping roof has a marble balustrade and a slender open-work spire 246 feet high. Two more towers with spires stand on each side of the façade, in front of which is a porch; above the porch is a great rose window with cusp (late 15th century), with themes from the Apocalypse.

Lower Church. Barely 23 feet high, it has an enormous nave compared with the two much smaller aisles at the sides. Trefoil arch motifs supported by slender shafts recur around the walls. The **apse** at the end is polygonal. The dominating note of the chapel is its extremely rich polychrome decoration.

Upper Church. It is reached by means of an internal staircase. Without aisles, it is 55 feet wide and 67 feet high. A high plinth runs all around the church, punctuated by open-work marble arcades which from time to time open onto deep niches. In the third bay are the two niches reserved for the king and his family. On each pier is a 14th-century statue of an Apostle. All the architectural elements of the church are thus reduced to a minimum, so as to leave room for the fifteen huge *stained-glass windows,* nearly 50 feet high, which with their 1134 scenes cover a surface of some 6650 square feet. They date from the 13th century and depict, in vivid, glowing colours, scenes from the New and Old Testaments.

Pont-au-Change and the Conciergerie in the background.

CONCIERGERIE

This severe building dates back to the time of Philippe the Fair, that is, to between the end of the 13th and the beginning of the 14th centuries. The name Conciergerie derives from *concierge,* the Royal governor who had charge of the building. Today it occupies the north wing of the Palais de Justice. From the Quai de la Mégisserie, the side of the building can be admired in all its beauty, with its twin towers: on the right the **Tour d'Argent,** where the Crown jewels were kept, and on the left the **Tour de César.** From the 16th century, the Conciergerie was a State prison: during the Revolution thousands and thousands of prisoners condemned to death were kept in its cells, including Marie-Antoinette, the sister of the king, Madame Elisabeth, Charlotte Corday and the poet André Chenier.

INTERIOR *(The entrance is at no. 1 Quai de l'Horloge)* — On the ground floor is the **Hall of the Guards,** with massive piers supporting Gothic vaults, and the huge **Hall of the Men-at-Arms.** The latter room, which has four aisles and is no less than 224 feet long, 88 feet wide and 26 feet high, was once the dining-hall of the king. From the nearby kitchens, with four enormous fireplaces in the corners, banquets could be prepared for at least a thousand guests. In a large room with cross vaults, prisoners could have, for a certain fee, straw pallets on which to pass the night; in another area, with the tragically ironic name of *Rue de Paris,* the poor prisoners were quartered. The most evocative cell is without doubt the one occupied from 2 August to 16 October 1793 by Marie-Antoinette; it was converted into a chapel in 1816 by the only remaining daughter of Louis XVI, the Duchess of Angoulême. The cell now communicates with the one occupied first by Danton and later by Robespierre. From here one reaches the **Girondins' Chapel,** which was converted into a collective prison: here the crucifix of Marie-Antoinette is kept. From the chapel one reaches in turn the **Womens' Courtyard,** in which female prisoners were imprisoned.

ÎLE ST-LOUIS

Returning to the top end of the Cité and crossing the modern bridge, Pont St-Louis, we reach the Île St-Louis, a place which retains its ancient fascination. A walk along its Quai d'Orléans leads to the **Polish Library** and the small **Adam-Mickiewicz Museum,** containing important relics of the life of Chopin, at no. 6. Further on, at no. 12, a medallion recalls the birth of the poet Arvers. Passing by the **Pont de la Tournelle,** originally built as a wooden bridge in 1370 but rebuilt several times and bearing a statue of *St Geneviève,* the patron saint of Paris, we reach the **church of St-Louis-en-l'Île.** This was begun in 1664 to a design by Le Vau but completed only in 1726; the interior has three aisles and is a splendid Baroque creation, with a wealth of gold, enamelwork and polychrome marbles.

Coming out of the church, we pass the Pont Sully to reach the end of the island, occupied by the Henri IV Square, a tiny garden with the *monument to the sculptor A. L. Barye.* Continuing along the Quai d'Anjou, we find the island's finest mansions. At no. 2 is the **Hôtel Lambert,** built in 1640 by Le Vau and decorated by Le Brun and Le Sueur; at no. 17 is the entrance to the **Hôtel de Lauzun,** one of the most luxurious examples of a private 17th-century dwelling. It was built in 1657 to Le Vau's plans, and belonged to the Duke of Lauzun (from whom it took its name) for only three years. Théophile Gautier founded the "Club des Haschischins" there and lived in the building with the other great poet, Charles Baudelaire. Today the building belongs to the City of Paris, which uses it for important official guests. At no. 27 Quai d'Anjou is the residence of the Marquise de Lambert, who created a literary circle here. From this point we walk along the Quai de Bourbon to the other end of the island.

> **GRAND LOUVRE** (Métro: Line 1 - Palais Royal and Musée du Louvre stations).
>
> Opening times: open everyday except Tuesday from 9 to 18 hours. On Wednesday (all the museum) and Monday (Richelieu wing), open until 22 hours.
> Entrances: main entrance in the Pyramid in the Cour Napoléon. Other entrances: Jaujard door in the Flora pavilion; Richelieu passage (groups) and Carrousel du Louvre.

GRAND LOUVRE

HISTORY — The origin of the Louvre goes back to the end of the 12th century, when Philippe Auguste, before leaving for the Third Crusade, had a fortress built near the river to defend Paris from the incursions of the Saxons (in fact the name Louvre seems to derive from the Saxon word "leovar", meaning "fortified dwelling"): this original nucleus occupied about a quarter of the present-day Cour Carrée. The king continued to live on the Cité, so that the fortress was used to contain the Treasury and the archives. In the 14th century, Charles V, knows as Charles the Wise, decided to make it his residence and had the famous Library constructed. But the kings did not live in the Louvre again until 1536, when François I, after having the old fortress knocked down, erected on its foundations a palace more in keeping with Renaissance tastes. Work proceeded under Henri II and Catherine de' Medici, who gave Philibert Delorme the task of constructing the Tuileries Palace and uniting it to the Louvre by means of an arm stretching out towards the Seine. The modifications and extensions to the palace continued under Henri IV, who had the Pavillon de Flore constructed, and under Louis XIII and Louis XIV, who completed the Cour Carrée and had the western façade with the

LOUVRE — **Le Pavillon de l'Horloge**   **The new ''Grand Louvre''**

Colonnade erected. In 1682, when the royal court was transferred to Versailles, work was virtually abandoned and the palace fell into such a state of ruin that in 1750 its demolition was even contemplated. But work on the palace, suspended during the Revolution, was resumed by Napoleon I: his architects, Percier and Fontaine, began building the north wing, finished in 1852 by Napoleon III, who finally decided to complete the Louvre. During the period of the Commune, in May 1871, the Tuileries Palace was burnt down and the Louvre assumed its present appearance. After the important Library of Charles the Wise had been dispersed, it was François I who, in the 16th century, first began an art collection. This was considerably enlarged under Louis XIII and Louis XIV, so much so that by the death of the latter the Louvre was already used regularly for exhibitions of paintings and sculptures. On 10 August 1793 it was opened to the public and its gallery thus finally became a museum. From then on, the collection was continually enlarged: Napoleon I went so far as to demand a tribute in works of art from the nations he conquered. The objects listed in the museum's catalogue today are subdivided into various sections: from ancient Egyptian, Greek and Roman to Oriental works, from medieval to modern sculpture, and from the objets d'art such as those belonging to the Royal Treasury to the immense collections of paintings.

THE MUSEUM

The starting point of the "Grand Louvre" project was the decision made by the President of the Republic, Mitterrand, in 1981, to restore the Louvre palace to its former function as a museum; and the first step was to move the Ministry of Finance, then based in the Flora Pavilion, to Bercy. Furthermore, in order to increase the exhibition area and connect the Louvre and the city more closely, new spaces were created under the Cour Napoléon. The link between the new rooms and the ground above is the magnificent light structure of the glass pyramid, flanked by two smaller pyramids that, as does the larger one, reflect the changing light of the Parisian sky in their transparency.

The author of this daring project which has been the cause of much discussion both by Parisians and others, is Ieoh Ming Pei, an American architect of Chinese origin who was already responsible for the construction of the new wing of the National Gallery in Washington.

The definitive transformation of the Louvre from palace to museum took place on the 20th November 1993, two hundred years after the Louvre was first opened to the public, with the inauguration of the Richelieu wing.

The Richelieu wing, with its 6 collections distributed in 22,000 square metres divided into 165 rooms, on four floors, can be said to be the new face of the Louvre, characterised by a new reading of the works of art and by a different kind of pleasure given by the exhibition spaces.

The reorganisation of the Richelieu wing has also involved the modification of what were the old Ministry of Finance car parks. Thanks to the wonderful transformation of the two courts and the fact that they have been covered (with a superb glass structure 30 metres tall), all the monumental statues of the French school created for outdoors (squares, parks and public gardens) can be exhibited here. These two

A partial view of the Pyramid; the Cour Puget seen from the Richelieu passage and the Richelieu wing seen through Pei's Pyramid.

Part of the Charles V walls and the "upside down pyramid"
in the underground Carrousel space.

A view of the Cour Puget.

courts, the Cour Puget and the Cour Marly (the first, 1800 square metres and the second 2150 sq.m.) have kept their original side entrance, so that it is possible to look down into them from the Richelieu Passage even if one is simply passing by.

A description of the total renovation of the museum must include the Carrousel Passage . It was designed by the architects Michel Macary and Gérard Grandval and is characterised by a central upside down pyramid, also the work of Pei, which lights the underground space and creates a sort of logical continuity with the Napoléon Hall. The windows of many shops (fashion, cosmetics, perfume, jewelry, records, books) face onto these vast galleries which converge on the pyramid. There are, furthermore, banks, restaurants, a chemist and a post office.

From this space it is possible to see the remains of the ancient Louvre of the Capetian era, built by Philip Augustus as a fortress, in the centre of which was an impressive round keep, 30 metres high and surrounded by a deep ditch. The truncated cone which formed the base, diameter fifteen metres, seven metres high, is in an excellent state of preservation.

The large dining room in the apartments of Napoleon III in the Richelieu wing and one of the human-headed bulls of the Cour Khorsabad.

A partial view of room 31 with, on the right, the gilded silver statue
of Peace by Chaudet.

In the light of all these new modifications and changes, the
Louvre museum is divided into the following 7 departments: **Oriental Antiquities and Islamic Art; Egyptian
Antiquities; Greek, Etruscan and Roman Antiquities;
Objets d'art; Sculpture; Graphic Arts; Paintings.**
These departments are arranged in three wings which are
reached by means of an escalator from the Napoléon Hall
under the large pyramid: the **Richelieu wing** which runs
along Rue de Rivoli; the **Denon wing** which runs parallel to
the Seine; the **Sully wing** which runs round the Cour
Carrée. In order to visit the various collections, the route
marked with different colours on the plans on page 39
must be followed.
The mezzanine of the Sully wing with the **mediaeval
Louvre** and the History of the Louvre must also be added to
these exhibition spaces.

VISIT TO THE COLLECTIONS

Oriental Antiquities and Islam: Richelieu wing (mezzanine and ground floor) and Sully wing (ground floor).

Egyptian Antiquities: Sully wing (mezzanine, ground floor and first floor).

Greek, Etruscan and Roman Antiquities: Denon wing (ground floor) and Sully wing (ground floor and first floor).

Objets d'art: Richelieu wing (first floor, where the *Apartments of Napoleon III* are also to be found: open to the public for the first time they are a perfect and rare decorative unity from the Second Empire); Sully wing (first floor) and Denon wing (first floor).

Sculpture: Richelieu wing (mezzanine and ground floor) and Denon wing (mezzanine and ground floor).

Pictures: Richelieu wing (second floor, French pictures from the XIVth to the XVIIth century and Dutch, Flemish and German pictures); Sully wing (second floor, French pictures from the XVIIth to XIXth century) and Denon wing (first floor, large size nineteenth century French pictures, Italian and Spanish pictures).

Graphic Arts: Richelieu wing (second floor, North schools); Sully wing (second floor, French school) and Delon wing (first floor, Italian school).

Mediaeval Louvre.

Thanks to the new Richelieu wing it has been possible to allow certain large cycle of works the right exhibition space, above all the 24 paintings dedicated to the life of Marie de' Medici, commissioned from Rubens by the Queen of France in 1622: inaugurated in 1625, they were initially conceived for the west gallery of the Luxembourg Palace. The **Medici Gallery** which holds them today is a vast space of 524 square metres, covered by a barrel vault and lit, as are the other rooms in this section, by zenithal light which caresses the pictures without ever striking them violently.

Prominence is also rightly given to another group of works, the 12 tapestries depicting the **Hunts of Maximilian**, woven in Brussels around 1530 from designs by Bernaert van Orley. Nor must the **Khorsabad Court** (Oriental Antiquities, room 4) be forgotten, it is a splendid and exciting reconstruction of the Palace of King Sargon II at Dur Sharrukin, what is now the town of Khorsabad, near Mosul.

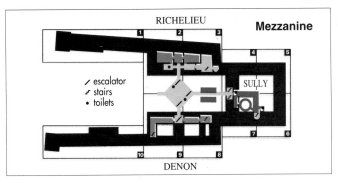

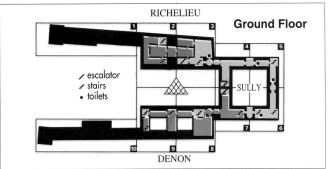

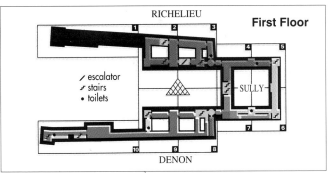

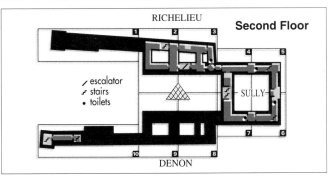

THE LOUVRE MUSEUM – Egyptian Art: **A relief with Seti I and the goddess Hathor;** a group with queen Hatshepsut and Senynefer, a gold pectoral and enamels of XIX dinasty.

ORIENTAL ANTIQUITIES

The Oriental Antiquities section, set up in 1881, is rich in exhibits and incorporates the vast zone which stretches from Bosphorus to the Persian Gulf.

The neo-Sumerian statues, which stylistically continue the previous Akkad dynasty period, are important: of these, a group of around thirty specimens representing *Gudea*, the "patési" of the city of Lagash, a dignitary who held political and religious offices, stand out. The majority of these statues come from Tello, discovered during French excavations: one of the objects, beautiful in the simplicity of its conception, is the one bought by the Louvre in 1953. Made from dolerite, it is 1.05 metres high and can be dated between 2290 and 2255 B.C. In a praying position, with his hands together, Gudea wears the typical Persian lamb hat on his head and a simple cloak over his shoulders. From the Mari excavations comes a small *statue in alabaster depicting the official, Ebih-il*, sitting with his hands together on a wicker stool: such chairs are still used today in Iraq. Of extraordinary importance not only as a work of art but also as a historical document, is the famous *Stele of Hammurabi* (beginning of 2nd millennium), a block of black basalt, 2.25 metres high, with the 282 laws which made up the legislative regulations and customs of the ancient Sumerians inscribed in the Akkadian language: these laws influenced the Justinian and Napoleonic Codes. There is some extremely beautiful evidence of Assyrian strength between the IX and VII centuries: for instance, the decorations of the Nimrud, Nineveh and Khorsabad palaces, with the grandiose, four metres high, *winged bulls* with human head; the *archers* of the Emperor's private guard, the so-called Immortals, come from the magnificent palace of Darius at Susa: each one is 1.47 metres high and they are made of glazed brick and painted. Mesopotamia, in fact, had little stone and thus always used bricks baked in the sun and then glazed. Finally, there are the antiquities from Palestine and the Syrian-Phoenician region up to its furthest points, Tunisia and Algeria.

EGYPTIAN ANTIQUITIES

This universally famous department was founded by Jean-François Champollion, who first deciphered the hieroglyphics. The Egyptian section of the Louvre has been continually enriched by purchases and donations and now offers the widest documentation possible on the civilization which developped along the Nile, from the dawning of its birth to the Ptolemaic, Roman and Byzantine period.

The statuette of the *Seated Scribe* belongs to the Old Kingdom and was made during the 5th Dynasty, maybe around 2500 B.C. Found at Sakkarah in 1921, the statuette, 53 centimetres high, is made of painted limestone and the eyes are encrusted with hard stones: the cornea in white quartz, the iris in rock

crystal and the pupils in ebony. Animated by an intense internal life, the scribe appears to interrogate with his eyes, ready to begin his work on the roll of papyrus resting on his lap. The Louvre possesses all the decorated part of the *mastaba of Akhtihetep* (5th Dynasty), with scenes illustrating daily life and the famous head of a man called *"Salt Head"*, because of its severe expression. The *statue of the Chancellor Nakhti*, of a surprising realism and with the wood still bearing traces of the original colour, and the harmonious *Girl Bearing Offerings* in plastered wood, are from the Middle Kingdom (12th Dynasty). We should not forget the powerful naturalism of the works from the period of Akhen-Aton, the heretic pharaoh, such as his extraordinary *sandstone bust*, discovered by Henri Chevrier or the *Princess's Head,* characterized by a very long neck.

An entire section has been dedicated to *Coptic art*, with a rich documentation of cloths, tapestries, detached frescoes and architectural remains.

GREEK AND ROMAN ANTIQUITIES

Like the Egyptian one, this section offers an extraordinary panorama of artistic material from the archaic age to the late Roman Empire.

The masterpieces are so many and so famous that it is almost impossible to mention them all. For the archaic period it is enough to remember the *Lady of Auxerre*, the *Hera of Samos*, the discreet, ironic smile illuminating the face of the *Rampin Horseman*. The classical period is well represented by a fragment of the *Frieze of the Panathenaic Women*, from the Parthenon of the Acropolis at Athens: created in the Phidias workshop in the 5th century B.C., this exhibit at the Louvre is also known as the frieze of the Ergastine Women. Two sculptures have contributed to the fame of the Museum which hosts them: the *Winged Victory of Samothrace* and the *Venus de Milo*. The former, found in 1863, is in Parian marble and perhaps commemorates the successes of the natives of Rhodes in the war against Antiochus III. The latter was discovered in 1820 by a peasant on the island of Milo in the Cyclades. It is dated around the end of the 2nd century B.C. Although it certainly derives from a Praxiteles original, it has become the prototype of Greek female beauty. Roman art is represented, amongst others, by the *frieze from the Ara Pacis* in Rome (9 B.C.); a statue depicting *Augustus* (considered to be one of the finest portraits of the Emperor); a series of *portraits of Trajan, Hadrian, Antoninus Pius*.

Apart from the bronzes, with the outstanding beauty of the *Apollo of Piombino,* there is the Greek-Roman jewellery, with the famous *Boscoreale Treasure,* found in a villa destroyed in 79 A.D. by the eruption of Vesuvius.

PAINTING COLLECTIONS

The collection of paintings at the Louvre is no doubt the best in the world and was started by François I (1515-1547). This sovereign began a true and proper collection of all types of works, destined to enrich the royal residence at Fontainebleau. He managed to secure the most famous artist of that time, Leonardo da Vinci and thus the possession of some of his most important works, such as the Mona Lisa and the Virgin of the Rocks. A further impetus was given to the collections by Louis XIII, although the true collector was not the King but his Minister, Cardinal Richelieu, who left everything to the Crown when he died. The collection was still relatively modest: an estimate made at the time numbered the paintings at 200. A real step forward came with the next King, Louis XIV, who bought part of Cardinal Mazarino's collection and the collection of Charles I of England. The collection grew further at the end of the 1700s, following requisitions from Churches, noble families or dissolved associations. Even though many works had been returned to their rightful owners by the end of 1815, from the Second Empire onwards, a wise purchasing policy consented continual enrichment with works of ever increasing importance, thus constantly enlarging the collections.

THE FRENCH SCHOOL

The paintings of the French school are, naturally, the most numerous of the whole picture gallery.
Amongst the masterpieces there is the *Villeneuve-lès-Avignon Pietà*, attributed to Enguerrand Quarton, an international Gothic masterpiece; the portraits include the *portrait of King Jean le Bon*, painted by an anonymous artist around 1360, and the splendid *portrait of Charles VII*, the "très victorieux" sovereign, painted by Jean Fouquet in 1444. The 16th century sees the splendid art of Jean and François Clouet (the latter was court painter in 1540) and that of the Fontainebleau School, a very refined example of which is the painting depicting the *Duchess of Villars and Gabrielle d'Estrée*. The works of the three Le Nain brothers, Antoine, Louis and Mathieu, are also very interesting: Louis is considered to be the best, far removed from the pomp of the court he specialized in portraying rustic scenes such as the *Peasant Family*, painted around 1643; of considerable interest is Georges de la Tour who, in his *St Joseph the Carpenter* or *Mary Magdalene with Oil-lamp*, shows Caravaggian influences, following a visit to Rome. The Roman lesson can also be seen in Nicolas Poussin's *Arcadian Shepherds* and *Rape of the Sabine Women* as well as Claude Lorrain's *Sea Port* and, above all, *Campo Vaccino in Rome*, which is full of the golden light typical of a sleepy afternoon at the Roman Forum. *Ex-Voto* by Philippe de Champaigne, is in perfect agreement with the artist's Jansenist ideals; it was painted between 22nd January and 15th June 1662, to thank

God for the miraculous healing of his paralysed daughter. In contrast with the serenity and mysticism of this composition is the opulence of the *Portrait of Chancellor Séguier*, painted by Charles Le Brun and clearly inspired by the models of the Italian 16th century.

Antoine Watteau most highly expressed Rococo: his *Embarkation for the Island of Cythera* which was much discussed because of its difficult interpretation, should be remembered, as well as the luminary *Gilles*, maybe painted around 1717 or 1719. The triumph of French Rococo was mainly due, however, to François Boucher, whose frequent descriptions of Venus were defined as "Boudoir Venuses" (eg. *Diana at Rest after Bathing*) and Jean-Honoré Fragonard, Boucher's pupil, with his sensual colours and full shapes *(the Bathers)*. Then, in agreement with the enthusiasm and admiration for antiquity, there is the domination of Louis David's neoclassicism: *Oath of the Horatii*, a true and proper manifestation of the new pictorial creed, the *Portrait of Madame Récamier*, of great purity and acute psychological introspection, and the *Coronation of Napoleon I*, a huge painting, 54 metres square, which definitively consacrated the artist as the first painter of the new Empire. In spite of the strong 16th century influence, Pierre Paul Prud'hon's *Transportation of Psyche* preannounces the themes used in Romanticism. Romanticism in fact explodes with Théodore Géricault who, inspired by a tragic and famous event (the shipwreck in 1816 of a French frigate carrying settlers to Senegal), painted the *Raft of the Medusa* in 1819, where the diagonal composition is just a tangled heap of disjointed bodies with hallucinated and dramatic faces. The work of the other great Romantic artist, Eugène Delacroix, should be placed next to that of Géricault: the Museum possesses some of his greatest paintings such as the famous *Liberty Guiding the People,* a true and proper manifestation of political propaganda; or *Death of Sardanapalus,* where the colours in the painting recall his long stays in Spain and Marocco; or the *Conquest of Jerusalem by the Crusaders* and the *Women of Algiers*. These two artists are contrasted by Jean-Auguste Ingres who opposes their colours with the purity of his fine and sinuous lines and refined curves: just observe the *Grande Odalisque* or the *Turkish Bath*, the latter inspired by the description of a harem in Lady Montague's letters. The Louvre possesses over 130 paintings by another famous artist, Camille Corot.

His *Woman with Pearl*, painted in 1868 in the pose of the Mona Lisa, is almost a prototype for all of his portraits: a still and quiet drawing with a sense of calm and serenity characterizes all of his works, be they portraits or landscapes.

THE LOUVRE MUSEUM – J. L. David: **Portrait of Madame Récamier**.

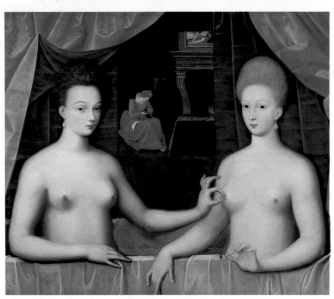

THE LOUVRE MUSEUM – The Fontainebleau School: **The Duchess of Villars and Gabrielle d'Estrées**.

THE ITALIAN SCHOOL

Of all the foreign schools at the Louvre, the Italian one is without doubt the best represented, featuring some true and proper masterpieces. The best of Florentine painting is present with the solemn *Majesty* by Cimabue, who perpetuates the Byzantine inspiration with rigorous symmetry and steady gestures, as well as the *altar steps of St Francis*, by Giotto. The 15th century is exalted by the *Coronation of the Virgin* by Fra Angelico; an episode of the *Battle of San Romano* by Paolo Uccello; the pure *Portrait of a Noblewoman of the Este Family* by Pisanello and works by Antonello da Messina *(Condottiero)* and Andrea Mantegna (a monumental *St Sebastian* and geometrical *Crucifixion*). The genius of Leonardo shines at the Louvre with three of his most beautiful works which are famous throughout the world: *St Ann with the Virgin and Child and Lamb*, painted between 1506 and 1510 for the high altar of the Church of the Servites in Florence; the *Virgin of the Rocks*, mysterious and cleverly constructed; the *Mona Lisa*, painted between 1503 and 1505 and so loved by the artist that he always took it with him, until it was sold in France to François I, either by Leonardo himself or by Melzi. This painting was the prototype for Renaissance portrait-painting and became even more famous when it was stolen from the Salon Carré in 1911 and found two years later in Florence. Some other great Italian works are the *Belle Jardinière* and *Portrait of Baldassarre Castiglione* by Raphael; the *Woman at the Mirror, Open-air Concert* and *Entombment of Christ*, by Titian; *the Wedding at Cana* by Veronese, an enormous painting where the artist inserts a crowd of over one hundred people under a typically Palladian architecture. Also present are *Hunting* and *Fishing* by Carracci; Caravaggio's *Death of the Virgin*, of a great realism and Francesco Guardi's series of paintings in honour of Alvise Mocenigo.

THE FLEMISH AND DUTCH SCHOOL

With regard to this collection, the Louvre possesses one of the most beautiful and important examples, the *Vergine d'Autun* by Jan van Eyck, also known as the Virgin of Chancellor Rolin, which is revolutionary for the open landscape behind the two main characters. Apart from the *Triptych of the Braque Family* by Rogier van der Weyden, attention should also be paid to the *Portrait of an Old Woman*, painted by Hans Memling around 1470-75; the *Banker and his Wife*, a typical painting of its kind, by Quentin Metsys, 1514; and the *Cripples* by Pieter Brueghel the Elder, an oil painting of small dimensions (18 by 21) and of great emotional content. This group of five unfortunates shows a bit of everything: the comparison of the various social classes, the symbol of the sins of humanity and the depiction of the revolt of the "gueux" of the Netherlands against the Spanish government of Philip II. The Flemish

LOUVRE MUSEUM – Charles Le Brun: **Portrait of Chancellor Séguier.**

THE LOUVRE MUSEUM – J. A. Ingres: **The Large Odalisque.**

LOUVRE MUSEUM – Eugène Delacroix: **Liberty guiding the People.**

LOUVRE MUSEUM – J. L. David: **Coronation of Napoleon I.**

School of the 17th century revolved around Peter Paul Rubens. His 21 majestic paintings on the *Life of Maria de' Medici* should be noted as well as the delicate *Portrait of his Wife Hélène Fourment* and the dazzling *Kermesse*, where he admirably blends the colour experience of the Venetians with the Flemish tradition for open air dancing. The 17th century is also similarly represented by the "King's painter" Antoine van Dyck: his *Portrait of Charles I*, due to its absorbed psychological introspection, began and was the prototype in England for a deeply rooted tradition.

The Dutch School is also represented by great masters: Hieronymus Bosch with the *Ship of Fools;* Luke of Leyda; Frans Hals, who reveals frequent contacts with northern Caravaggism in the *Bohémienne;* Johannes Vermeer, who transports us into the intimate surroundings of bourgeois houses: in the *Lacevendor* (painted between 1664 and 1665), the perfect agreement between the lights, volumes and colours, transfigures the character from simplicity raising it to the highest levels of absolute values. And finally there is the glorious and numerous collection of works by Rembrandt, especially his portraits and self-portraits. We should particularly remember the *Self-Portrait* painted in 1660, *Bathsheba* and *Supper at Emmaus* in which the artist, at the height of his maturity, attains highly dramatic and mystical effects.

Although more modest, the German collection contains valuable works such as *Self-Portrait* by Dürer, *Venus* by Cranach and *Portrait of Erasmus*, painted in 1523 by Hans Holbein the Younger. He also painted the *Portrait of Anne of Cleves* and the *Portrait of Nikolaus Kratzer.*

THE ENGLISH SCHOOL

England is represented at the Louvre by the great portrait-painters of the 17th century and first of all by Joshua Reynolds with his delicate and famous *Master Hare*, and Thomas Lawrence with the *Portraits of Julius Angerstein and his Wife*. The 19th century presents landscapes by Richard Parkes Bonington *(Mirror of Water at Versailles)*, John Constable *(Bay of Weymouth)* and Joseph Turner *(Sea at Margate)*.

THE SPANISH SCHOOL

The Spanish School has many prestigious works and is distinguished above all by the great painting of the *Crucifixion* by El Greco; the *St Apollonia* and *Funeral of St Bonaventura* by Zurbaran; the *Young Beggar* and *Miracle of St James* by Murillo; *Portraits of the Infante Marguerite* and *Queen Mariana* by Diego Velasquez and, finally, numerous portraits by Goya including *Woman with Fan* and above all the *Countess of Carpio*, one of his masterpieces painted around 1794, where the velvet black of the long skirt contrasts with the precious

LOUVRE MUSEUM – Leonardo da Vinci: **Mona Lisa**.

white lacework of the mantilla and the big pink ribbon, revealed by a few clever touches of light.

SCULPTURES

With regard to sculpture, it can be said that today the Louvre offers the most complete panorama of the history of sculpture from its origins up until the present day. We begin with the first Romanesque sculptures still closely linked to architectural functions, for instance decorated capitals, and then go on to

THE LOUVRE MUSEUM – J. B. Chardin: **Young Artist**.

THE LOUVRE MUSEUM – P. P. Rubens: **La Kermesse**.

THE LOUVRE MUSEUM – N. Poussin: **Inspiration of the poet**.

THE LOUVRE MUSEUM – F. Boucher: **Diana's Rest**.

THE LOUVRE MUSEUM – Titian: **Woman in the mirror**.

THE LOUVRE MUSEUM – C. Lorrain: **Cleopatra's Landing at Tarsus**.

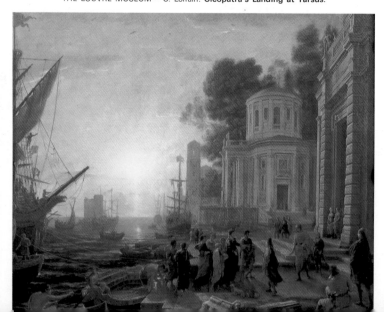

the first examples of statues which complete the concept of sculpture as we know it today. Then there is the wealth of Gothic, with sculptures from Chartres, Bourges and Rheims (in particular the *funeral statue of Marie Bourbon*), *the tomb of Philippe Pot* from the last quarter of the 15th century, created by Antoine le Moiturier for Citeaux Abbey. The Renaissance period is documented by the works of two great sculptors: Jean Goujon and Germain Pilon. Of the former we should remember the reliefs of the *Fountain of the Innocents* and the *Deposition from the Cross with Four Evangelists;* of the latter, there is the delicate group of the *Three Graces* and the statue of the *Cardinal of Birague in Prayer.* The 17th and 18th centuries are represented by works of Pierre Puget, whose *Milo of Crotona* expresses all of the artist's dramatic genius; Simon Guillan with his bronze statues of *Anne of Austria, Louis XIII* and *Louis XIV as a Boy*, created for the Pont-au-Change monument; Antoine Coysevox with his statue of the *Seine* and the vigorous *Bust of Louis II of Bourbon;* Falconet (with a very delicate *Bather*) and Jean Antoine Houdon, whose art goes from the slender bronze depicting *Diana* to the terracottas with which he modelled the *Bust of Benjamin Franklin* and the *Bust of Louise Brongniart as a Girl.* Finally, we should not forget the famous *Love and Psyche*, sculpted by Canova in 1793, with the joyful contrast of *The Dance* by Jean Baptiste Carpeaux (1869).

Italian sculpture is represented by works of Nino Pisano, the Della Robbia family, Agostino di Duccio, Benedetto da Maiano *(Bust of Filippo Strozzi)*, Jacopo della Quercia *(Virgin and Child)* and Desiderio da Settignano. Amongst the masterpieces there are *Rebellious Slave* and the *Dying Slave* by Michelangelo, sculpted between 1513 and 1515 for the tomb of Pope Julius II; Giambologna's *Mercury* and the *Nymph of Fontainebleau* by Benvenuto Cellini.

OBJETS D'ART

This section is of exceptional importance not only from an artistic but also a historical point of view. The most varied types of objects are gathered here, from furniture to tapestries, from jewellery to small bronzes, from miniatures to porcelains.

The Apollo Gallery, with the ceiling painted by Le Brun, hosts the Royal Treasury. Outstanding are the *Crown of St Louis*, the *Crown of Louis XV* and that of *Napoleon I;* the *broche-reliquary* made for the Empress Eugenia in 1855; the *Hortensia diamond* of 20 carats, the *Sancy diamond* of 55 carats and the splendid *Regent*, 136 carats, sent from Madras in England in 1702 by Thomas Pitt and bought for the French Crown in 1717 by the Duke of Orléans; and some pieces from the *Treasury of St Denis* and the *Treasury of the Order of St Esprit*, founded by Henry II in 1578.

Along the rooms of the Colonnade, there is the reconstruction of the Council Room from the Palace of Vincennes, the ceiling

THE LOUVRE MUSEUM – Michelangelo: **The rebellious slave and the dying slave**.

with the facings and doors of the King's Ceremonial Chamber at the Louvre; the ivory *Harbaville Triptych* from the middle of the 10th century; the *reliquary arm of St Louis of Toulouse* in crystal and gilded silver; the tapestries of the *Hunt of Maximilian*, woven in Brussels to a design by Van Orley in 1535 and the tapestry of the *Martyrdom of St Mames*, designed by Jean Cousin and woven by Pierre Blassé and Jacques Langlois; then, in the Room of the Marshal of Effiat, there are the Gobelins tapestries depicting *Stories of Scipio*, by Giulio Romano; furniture by the famous cabinet-maker, André-Charles Boulle; the splendid, unique collection of snuff boxes, boxes for sweets and other objects and clocks from the 17th and 18th centuries, decorated with chisel work, enamels, encrusted with precious stones and miniatures; the *writing desk of the King* by J. F. Oeben; the Chinese Room with a series of Chinese panels

58

THE LOUVRE MUSEUM – F. Rude: **Young Neapolitan fisherman playing with a turtle**; Falconet: **Bather**; A. Canova: **Love and Psyche**.

Carrousel Arch.

of painted paper from the end of the 18th century; Antoinette's dressing-case for travelling, made in Paris in 1787-88; the *Throne of Napoleon I*, made in 1804 and the *Cradle of the King of Rome*, made in 1811 to a design by Prud'hon; the Adolphe de Rothschild collection with a bas relief by Agostino di Duccio depicting the *Virgin and Child with Angels*; the Camondo collection, the Schlichting collection and the Thiers collection with 18th century porcelains, Japanese lacquer work and Chinese jade.

PLACE DU CARROUSEL — This garden occupies the site on which the Tuileries Palace stood before it was burnt down in 1871. The entrance portal is all that remains today of this magnificent palace. In 1964-1965 a sort of open-air museum was organised here, with many works of sculpture, among the most important being those by Aristide Maillol, including *Night* and the *Reclining Woman*.

CARROUSEL ARCH

Designed by Pierre-François Fontaine and Charles Percier, the arch was built between 1806 and 1808 and was intended to celebrate the victories of Napoleon Bonaparte in 1805. It imitates both the architectural design and the decoration of the Arch of Septimius Severus in Rome. Red and white marble columns frame the three archways and each side is filled with bas reliefs which recall the Emperor's victories. On top of it were placed the four gilded horses which had been removed by order of Napoleon from the Venetian basilica of San Marco, to which they were returned in 1815. The originals were then replaced by copies, and a chariot and the *statue of Peace* were added later.

ST-GERMAIN-L'AUXERROIS

Also called the "Grande Paroisse", the Great Parish Church, because it was the royal chapel of the Louvre in the 14th century, the present church of St-Germain stands on the site of a previous sanctuary dating from the Merovingian era. Its construction took from the 12th to the 16th century. On the façade is a deep porch in Gothic style (1435-1439), with five arches, each one different from the others, and statues adorning the pillars which divide them. Above the porch is the rose window, surmounted by a cusp, and alongside it the bell tower (11th century).

Interior. The church's interior is impressive, including nave and double aisles divided by pillars, transept and chancel. It contains a wealth of art works. Worth noting is the **royal pew,** carved from wood by F. Mercier in 1682. Also in polychrome wood is the *statue representing St Germanus,* while that of *St Vincent* is of stone; both are from the 15th century. A *Flemish altarpiece* in carved wood depicts scenes from the life of Christ.

ST. GERMAIN-L'AUXERROIS — **General view of the Church.**

PLACE DES PYRAMIDES – **Equestrian statue of Joan of Arc.**

RUE DE RIVOLI — This street runs parallel to the Seine between Place de la Concorde and Place de la Bastille. It owes its name to the victory which Napoleon won against Austria at Rivoli in 1797. Elegant porticoes line the right-hand side of the street.

PLACE DES PYRAMIDES — This small square lies in front of the Pavillon de Marsan; in the centre is the *equestrian statue of Joan of Arc* (Frémiet, 1874), to which on 12 May every year many people make a pilgrimage.

MUSEUM OF DECORATIVE ARTS — Entrance at no. 107 Rue de Rivoli. It contains about 50,000 pieces, which illustrate the evolution of taste and form in painting, sculpture, furnishing and allied arts.

Ground floor. Here temporary exhibitions of great importance are held. On the **first floor** are the collections belonging to the Gothic and Renaissance periods, including tapestries, sculpture, pottery, arms and musical instruments. The **second floor** is dedicated to the collections from the eras of Louis XV and the Directory: here too there is such a wealth of objects that an exact reconstruction of French life in these periods can be made. The **third floor** is reserved for the decorative arts of other countries: Italy, Germany, Russia and England. There are also pieces from the art of Asia Minor, India, China, Japan, Persia, etc.

PALAIS ROYAL

Constructed by Lemercier between 1624 and 1645, this palace was originally the private residence of Cardinal Richelieu, who on his death in 1642 left it to Louis XIII. Today it is the seat of the Council of State. It has a façade with columns erected in 1774 and a small courtyard from which one passes through a double colonnade into a splendid and famous garden. This garden was planned by Louis in 1781 and extends for some 250 yards. Three wings of robust pillars surround it, and the portico thus formed is occupied

Palais Royal.

today by extremely interesting shops selling old objects and rare books. During the Revolution, it became the meeting-place of patriots: in fact here the anti-monarchical nobles met, and among this group was the Duke of Orléans, who was later to rename himself Philippe-Egalité.

BANK OF FRANCE – This stands to the right of the Palais Royal, with its entrance at no. 39 Rue Croix-des-Petits-Champs. It was founded by order of Napoleon in January 1800. The bank occupies part of a building erected by Mansart in 1638: in it is the magnificent **Galerie Doré,** which can be visited only by scholars, a work by Robert de Cotte, with sculpture by Vassé, constructed in 1719. At a depth of some 60 feet is the steel and reinforced concrete strong-room which contains the reserves of the Bank.

PLACE DES VICTOIRES – This square, circular in form, came into being in 1685 as a surrounding for the allegorical statue of Louis XIV, commissioned from Desjardins by the Duke de la Feuillade. The statue was later destroyed during the Revolution and replaced by another, made by Bosio, in 1822. The square was created under the direction of Jules Hardouin-Mansart, and important figures came to live here: the Duke de la Feuillade himself occupied nos. 2 and 4, while the financier Crosat lived at no. 3.

NOTRE-DAME-DES-VICTOIRES – The church belonged to a monastery of the Barefooted Augustinians. The foundation stone was laid by Louis XIII in 1629, but it was not completed until 1740. Important pilgrimages to the Virgin have been held here since 1836, and in the church there are more than 30,000 ex voto offerings.

Interior. It is without aisles, but has linking chapels along the sides. In the second chapel on the left is the *tomb* of the Florentine composer Lulli, who died in 1687. In the chancel are 17th-century wood carvings and seven canvases by Van Loo, depicting scenes from the life of St Augustine and Louis XIII as he dedicates the church to the Virgin.

NATIONAL LIBRARY

The main entrance is at no. 58 Rue de Richelieu (in front of the Square Louvois, with its fine fountain made by Visconti in 1844). This is one of the richest libraries in the world: it occupies an area of some 180,000 square feet and its possessions are divided into seven sections. Thanks to aquisitions, copyright deposits, donations and so on, the library today has about seven million volumes (among them two editions of the Gutemberg Bible). It also has 250,000 complete collections of periodicals and newspapers, 12 million prints (the richest collection in the world), 900,000 musical works (including scores and manuscripts), and finally what is considered its most precious section, containing original manuscripts of Victor Hugo and Proust and extremely important miniatures such as the *Gospel of Charlemagne,* the *Bible of Charles the Bald,* the *Psalter of St Louis* and the *Rich Hours of the Duke of Berry.* The library also contains the **Medals and Antiques Section,** in which are kept coins and medals from all different periods and the treasures of St-Denis and of the Sainte-Chapelle.

From the entrance one passes directly into the monumental courtyard, a work by Robert de Cotte (18th century). From here, on the right, one reaches the vestibule, where the finest

Place des Victoires.

books held by the libary under the copyright law are displayed. The vestibule leads in turn to the library's various departments. At the end is the **Galerie Mansart,** where important exhibitions are often held; opposite is the State Room, with the original plaster bust of Voltaire by Houdon. The monumental staircase leads up to the first floor, where the splendid **Mazarin Gallery,** designed by Mansart with paintings by G. F. Romanelli, is to be found.

PLACE DU THÉÂTRE FRANÇAIS — This colourful square lies at the end of the Avenue de l'Opéra. In it is France's most important prose theatre, the **Comédie-Française,** founded in 1680 by the merging of Molière's company of actors with those of the Hôtel de Bourgogne. In 1812, a special statute was created for the company by Napoleon (the "décret de Moscou"). The repertoire of the Comédie ranges from the French classics (Molière above all, followed by Racine, Corneille, etc.) to the modern French writers (Claudel and Anouihl), besides foreigners (Pirandello). The building was erected by Louis in 1786-1790, and its facade was added by Chabrol in 1850. In the vestibule and in the foyer can be seen the statues of the great dramatic writers: those of Voltaire and Molière (works by Houdon), Victor Hugo (by Dalou), Dumas (by Carpeaux) and others. Also to be seen is the chair in which Molière was sitting on stage, while acting in his Imaginary Invalid, when hit by a fatal illness on 17 February 1673.

RUE ST-HONORÉ – This is one of the oldest streets in Paris: in fact it existed as far back as the 12th century. Furthermore, it is a street filled with memories of the Revolution: the club of the Feuillants was here, and not far away the club of the Jacobins, headed by Robespierre. The street was also on the route along which the carts passed carrying those condemned to death from the Conciergerie prison to the guillotine in Place de la Concorde.

CHURCH OF ST-ROCH

In Rue St-Honoré, the church of St-Roch is extremely interesting because of the works of art it contains. It was begun under Louis XIV in 1653 and finished a century later; in 1736 the façade was erected by Robert de Cotte.
Interior. Built in a sumptuous Baroque style, it has three aisles with side chapels, transept, chancel and ambulatory with radial chapels; behind the chancel is a vast round chapel,

ST-ROCH – **Façade.**

the **Lady Chapel,** with a ring-shaped nave and semicircular apse (built by Hardouin-Mansart); and behind the Lady Chapel is a rectangular chapel, called the **Calvary Chapel.** The church contains the remains of many illustrious men: Corneille, Diderot, Le Nôtre and others.

RIGHT AISLE
1st chapel: *monument to Henri de Lorraine,* by Renard (17th century), and *bust of François de Créqui,* by Coysevox. **2nd chapel:** *funeral monument to the astronomer Maupertuis* (d'Huez) and *statue of Cardinal Dubois* (G. Coustou). **3nd chapel:** *tomb of Duke Charles de Créqui.*

LEFT AISLE
1st chapel: *frescoes by Chassériau* (19th century), depicting St Francis Saverius and St Philip. **2nd chapel:** *Baptism of Christ* by Lemoyne. **3rd chapel:** two works by Lemoyne, the *statue of his daughter* and a *bust of Mignard.* On the first pillar of the ambulatory on the left, a *bust of Le Nôtre* by Coysevox, and in the **5th chapel** the *monument to the Abbot de l'Epée.*

In the **Lady Chapel,** with its frescoes on the cupola painted by J. B. Pierre depicting the *Triumph of the Virgin,* other important works: on the altar, a *Nativity* by the Anguier brothers; on the pillar at left the *Resurrection of the Son of the Widow of Naim* by Le Sueur (17th century). On the first pillar of the left aisle is a plaque recalling that in this church, on 2 April 1810, Alessandro Manzoni, the great Italian novelist, rediscovered his faith.

PLACE VENDÔME

A vast architectural complex dating from the time of Louis XIV, its name derives from the fact that the residence of the Duke of Vendôme was here. It was created between 1687 and 1720 as a setting for the equestrian statue by Girardon dedicated to Louis XIV and destroyed during the Revolution. The square, octagonal in form, simple and austere, is surrounded by buildings which have large arcades on the ground floor and skilfully distributed pediments higher up, crowned on the roofs by the dormer-windows typical of Paris. Today at no. 15 is the famous Hôtel Ritz and at no. 12 the house where Chopin died in 1849. In the centre of the square is the **column** erected by Gondouin and Lepère between 1806 and 1810 in honour of Napoleon I. Inspired by the Column of Trajan in Rome, it is 145 feet high, and around its shaft is a spiralling series of bronze bas reliefs, cast from the 1200 cannon captured at Austerlitz. On the top of the column, Chaudet erected a statue of the Emperor dressed as Caesar, but it was destroyed in 1814 and replaced with a statue of Henri IV. It was replaced in 1863, this time in the military dress of the Little Corporal, but eight years later, at the time of the Commune, it was once more pulled down. It was

PLACE VENDÔME — **Column**.

finally replaced three years later by a copy of the original by Chaudet.

From Place Vendôme, we walk along **Rue de la Paix,** which was previously called Rue Napoléon. Today it is one of the most splendid streets in the city, lined by famous and expensive shops: at no. 13 is the jeweller Cartier. At the end of the street on the right we reach the **Avenue de l'Opéra,** which was opened at the time of the Second Empire.

OPÉRA

The Opéra is the largest theatre for lyric opera in the world (it covers an area of 120,000 square feet and can accommodate an audience of 2000 and 450 performers on the stage). Designed by Garnier and built between 1862 and 1875, it is the most typical monument of the era of Napoleon III.

Opéra.

An ample stairway leads up to the first of the two orders into which the façade is divided, with its large arcades and robust pillars, in front of which are numerous marble groups. The finest is the one in front of the second pillar on the right: **The Dance,** by Jean-Baptiste Carpeaux. The second order consists of tall double columns framing large windows; above is an attic, with exuberant decoration, on which the flattened cupola rests. The interior is just as highly adorned: its great staircase is enriched by marbles, the vault is decorated with paintings by Isidore Pils and the hall has a large fresco by Marc Chagall (1966).

The Opéra also stands at the beginning of the **Boulevard des Capucines,** so called because near here stood a convent of Capuchin nuns. At no. 28 is the **Olympia,** the famous music-hall; at no. 14 an epigraph recalls that here on 28 December 1895 the Lumière brothers projected a film for the first time in public. On the footpath here in 1842, in front of what is now the Ministry for Foreign Affairs, Stendhal collapsed after an apoplectic stroke. At no. 24 is the **Cognacq-Jay-Museum.** The building belonged to E. Cognacq, founder of the Samaritaine stores. The museum contains a collection of paintings, sculpture and works of art from the 18th century. It includes paintings by Canaletto, Guardi, Gainsborough, Reynolds, Boucher, Chardin, Fragonard, Rubens and Rembrandt.

MADELEINE

Designed along the lines of the Maison Carrée at Nîmes, the Madeleine was built by order of Napoleon in honour of the Grand Army. He had a previous building, which had never been completed, demolished and in 1806 commissioned the

The Madeleine.

architect Vignon to construct it. In 1814 it became a church and was dedicated to St Mary Magdalene. It has the form and structure of a classical Greek temple: a wide base, with a stairway and a colonnade of 52 Corinthian columns 65 feet high. The pediment has a huge frieze sculpted by Lemaire in 1834 and depicting the *Last Judgment*.

Interior. The building is without aisles. In the vestibule are two groups of sculpture by Pradier and Rude. Above the high altar is a work by Marochetti *(Assumption of St Mary Magdalene)*.

In front of the Madeleine, the **Rue Royale** stretches out in a fine perspective, closed at the other end by the symmetrical mass of the Palais Bourbon. The Rue Royale, opened in 1732, is short but full of luxury, including for example Maxim's restaurant and the shop of Christofle. At no. 6 Madame de Stael lived.

About halfway along Rue Royale is another important street, the **Rue du Faubourg St-Honoré,** of which the number 13 was removed by order of the superstitious Empress Eugénie. This street has become almost synonymous with elegance and fashion, since it contains some of the most famous shops for perfumes, jewellery and dresses in the world. Among their names are St Laurent, Hermes, Cardin, Lancôme, Helena Rubinstein and Lanvin.

ÉLYSÉE PALACE

This is the residence of the President of the French Republic. It was built in 1718 by Mollet for the son-in-law of the financier Crozat, the Count d'Evreux. After becoming public

Rue Royale.

property during the Revolution, it was inhabited by Caroline Bonaparte and later by the Empress Josephine. Here, on 22 June 1815, Napoleon signed his act of abdication. Since 1873 the Élysée has been the official residence of the various presidents who have headed the French Republic.

Élysée Palace.

ITINERARY 4

FROM PLACE DE LA CONCORDE *(Métro: lines 1, 8, 12 – Concorde station)* **TO PONT ALEXANDRE III.**

Place de la Concorde – Tuileries – Orangerie Museum – Orsay Museum – Champs-Élysées – Place de Gaulle – Arch of Triumph – Grand Palais – Petit Palais – Pont Alexandre III.

PLACE DE LA CONCORDE

Laid out by Jacques-Ange Gabriel between 1757 and 1779, the square was originally dedicated to Louis XV, of whom there was an equestrian statue in the centre by Pigalle and Bouchardon, pulled down during the Revolution. In its place the guillotine was erected, and among those who died here were King Louis XVI, his queen, Marie-Antoinette, Danton, Madame Roland, Robespierre and St Just. The square assumed its present appearance between 1836 and 1840, when it was replanned by the architect Hittorf. In the centre stands the **Egyptian obelisk** from the temple of Luxor, given in 1831 by Mohammed Ali to Louis-Philippe and erected in 1836. It is 75 feet high and is adorned with hieroglyphics which illustrate the deeds of the pharaoh Rameses II. At the corners of the square are the eight statues which symbolise the main cities of France. On the northern side, the two colonnaded buildings (designed by Gabriel) today contain the **Ministry of the Navy** and the **Hôtel Crillon.**

View of Place de la Concorde on the north side.

Place de la Concorde.

TUILERIES GARDENS

The gardens extend for about one kilometer between Place de la Concorde and Place du Carrousel. Entrance is through an imposing gate with pillars bearing the **equestrian statues of Mercury** (on the right) and **Fame** (on the left), both by Coysevox.

Two flights of steps lead up to the terraces of the Orangerie (to the right) and of the Jeune de Paume (to the left), which until recently housed the Impressionist collections now on display at the Orsay Museum on the left bank of the Seine. Nowadays temporary exhibitions are held at the Jeu de Paume.

ORSAY MUSEUM

What the press defined as "the most beautiful museum in Europe" is to be found on the left bank of the Seine, where the State Audit Court originally stood in 1870; it was then destroyed during the Commune. In 1898 the Paris-Orléans railway company assigned the building of the new station to Victor Laloux. The work was carried out in two years so that the Gare d'Orsay was ready for the universal exhibition held in 1900. Laloux designed a grandiose nave 135 metres by 40 metres, the metal structure of which was skilfully covered on the outside by light coloured stuccowork. The interior not only housed the sixteen platforms but also restaurants and an elegant hotel with at least 400 rooms. Abandoned in 1939, the Gare d'Orsay went on a

Musée d'Orsay on the left bank of the Seine.

Musée d'Orsay: view of the central hall.

slow decline under the spectre of demolition: Orson Welles's cultural revival with the filming of *The Trial* or the establishment of Jean-Louis Barrault's company there were of no avail. In 1973 the French President at the time, Georges Pompidou, declared it a national monument and saw to it that a museum displaying the half century of art that goes from Napoleon III's Second Empire to the beginnings of Cubism was up there. It proved to be a perfect link between the Louvre, a temple of

MUSEE D'ORSAY – Van Gogh: The Church at Auvers.

ancient art, and the Centre Georges Pompidou, a temple of modern art. The tender for contract for its restructuring commenced in 1978 and was won by the ACT group; the Italian architect, Mrs. Gae Aulenti, was entrusted with the interior decorating. Nowadays more than 4,000 works including paintings, sculptures, drawings and furniture are exhibited in over 45,000 square metres.

The **ground floor** features paintings, sculptures and decorative arts from 1850 to 1870, with works by Ingres, Delacroix, Manet, Puvis de Chavannes and Gustave Moreau whereas Impressionist paintings (Monet, Renoir, Pissarro, Degas and Manet), Personnaz, Gachet and Guillaumin collections and Post-Impressionist paintings with masterpieces by Seurat, Signac, Toulouse-Lautrec, Gauguin, Van Gogh and the Nabis group (Bonnard, Vuillard and Vallotton) are displayed on the **top floor**. Lastly, the **middle floor** features art from 1870 to 1914, with the official art of the III Republic, Symbolism, academic painting and the decorative arts of the Art Nouveau period, with Guimard, Emile Gallé and the School of Nancy.

Champs-Élysées.

CHAMPS-ÉLYSÉES

This was originally a vast swampy area; after its reclamation, Le Nôtre in 1667 designed the wide avenue which was first called the Grand-Cours (its present name dates from 1709): it extends from the Tuileries to Place de l'Étoile, now now called Place de Gaulle. At the beginning of the avenue are the celebrated **Horses of Marly,** by Guillaume Coustou. From here to the Rond-Point of the Champs-Élysées, the

Champs-Élysées.

avenue is flanked by a vast park. As we walk along it, on the right is the **Théâtre des Ambassadeurs-Espace Pierre Cardin,** on the left the **Ledoyen restaurant** from the time of Louis XVI. In **Place Clemenceau** is the bronze *statue* of this famous politician who led France to victory in 1918. At this point the panoramic **Avenue Churchill** begins, with the Alexandre III Bridge and the Invalides in the background. On each side of the Avenue Churchill are the Grand Palais and the Petit Palais, two imposing buildings with large colonnades, friezes and sculptural groups, erected for the World Fair held in Paris in 1900.

ROND-POINT of the Champs-Élysées — This important intersection is at the end of the park zone of the Champs-Elysées; the square, about 150 yards wide, was designed by Le Nôtre. On the right is the headquarters of the newspaper Le Figaro, on the left that of Jours de France. This is the beginning of the wide street (its two footpaths some 25 yards wide and the roadway more than 30) along either side of which are the offices of airlines, banks and automobile showrooms. There are three large covered galleries, the **Galerie Elysées-La Boétie** at no. 54, the **Galerie Arcades** at no. 76 and the **Galerie Point-Show** at no. 66.

PLACE DE GAULLE

Formerly Place de l'Étoile, this square is at the end of the Champs-Élysées. It is a vast circular area 130 yards in diameter, from which a total of twelve important streets radiate out: Avenue des Champs-Élysées, Avenue de Friedland, Avenue Hoche, Avenue de Wagram, Avenue MacMahon, Avenue Carnot, Avenue de la Grande Armée, Avenue Foch, Avenue Victor Hugo, Avenue Kléber, Avenue d'Iena and Avenue Marceau.

Arch of Triumph.

ARCH OF TRIUMPH

The massive arch stands in majestic isolation in the centre of the square. Ordered by Napoleon as a memorial to the Grand Army, it was begun by Chalgrin in 1806. Completed in 1836, it has a single archway and actually exceeds in size the Arch of Constantine in Rome: it is 164 feet high and 147 feet wide. On the faces of the arch are bas reliefs, the best known and finest piece being that on the right, on the part of the arch facing the Champs-Élysées, depicting the departure of the volunteers in 1792 and known as the **Marseillaise** (F. Rude). The bas reliefs higher up celebrate the victories of Napoleon, while the shields sculpted on the attic bear the names of the great battles. Under the arch in 1920 the Tomb of the Unknown Soldier was placed and its eternal flame is tended every evening. In a small museum inside the arch itself there is a history of the monument.

Grand Palais.

GRAND PALAIS

It was built by Daglone and Louvet and has a façade with
Ionic columns 787 feet long and 65 feet high. Today art
shows, including important exhibitions of painting, are held
here. Part of it is occupied by the **Palais de la Découverte,**
or Palace of Discovery, where the most recent conquests of
science and the steps in man's progress are celebrated.

PETIT PALAIS

This contains the Musée du Petit Palais, a large collection
of ancient and modern art. It includes paintings by French
artists of the 19th and 20th centuries (from Géricault to
Delacroix, from Ingres to Courbet, from Redon to Bonnard),
which are part of the **Municipal Collections.** The **Tuck
and Dutuit collections,** on the other hand, include not
only various objects of Greek, Roman, Etruscan and Egyptian
antiquity (among them enamelwork and pottery), but also
drawings and paintings from various eras and various countries
(including Dürer, Cranach, Van de Velde, Watteau, Pollaiolo,
Guardi).

ALEXANDRE III BRIDGE

This is at the end of the Avenue Winston Churchill. It consists
of a single metal span, 350 feet long and 130 feet wide,
linking the Esplanade des Invalides and the Champs-Élysées.

It was built between 1896 and 1900 to celebrate the alliance between Russia and France, and is named after Czar Alexander III, whose son, Nicholas II, performed its inauguration. On the two piers on the right bank are the statues representing medieval France and modern France, while those on the left bank represent Renaissance France and the France of Louis XIV. On the bridge's entrance piers are the allegories of the rivers Seine and Neva, symbolising France and Russia. The whole bridge has exuberant decorations with cherubs, allegorical marine deities, garlands of flowers and lamps supported by cherubs.

Detail of piers on Alexander III Bridge.

ITINERARY 5

FROM THE GUIMET MUSEUM *(Métro: line 9 – Iéna station)* **TO THE RODIN MUSEUM.**

Guimet Museum – Palais Galliera – Musée de la Mode et du Costume – Palais de Tokyo – Museum of Modern Art of the City of Paris – Place du Trocadéro – Passy Cemetery – Clemenceau Museum – Maison de Radio-France – **Palais de Chaillot** – **Eiffel Tower** – **Champ-de-Mars** – **Military Academy** – Maison de l'U.N.E.S.C.O. – **Les Invalides** – Rodin Museum.

We now move on to the Chaillot quarter, which we reach via the Avenue d'Iéna as far as the square of the same name. In the centre is an **equestrian statue of George Washington,** a gift from the women of America. The modern building with rotunda on the corner of the square is now the headquarters of the Economic and Social Council (Perret, 1938).

GUIMET MUSEUM – Entrance at no. 6. Founded by the art collector Guimet from Lyons, it gives a complete panorama of the art of the East and Far East. It includes works of art from India (among them the **Cosmic Dance of Siva**), Cambodia (collection of Khmer art), Nepal, Tibet (**Dancing Dakini** in gilt bronze), Afghanistan, Pakistan, China and Japan.

PALAIS GALLIERA – This is nearby, its entrance at no. 10 Avenue Pierre Ier-de-Serbie. The building, Renaissance in style, was erected for the Duchess of Galliera in 1889 to house her art collections. These were eventually left to the city of Genoa, while the building was left to Paris. The museum now hosts the **Musée de la Mode et du Costume.**

MUSÉE DE LA MODE ET DU COSTUME – This museum's collections include 2000 costumes and more than 12,000 pieces, giving a complete panoramic view of the evolution of French fashion from 1735 to today.

PALAIS DE TOKYO – This is situated at no. 13 Avenue du Président Wilson and was built for the Exhibition of 1937. It consists of two separate sections, linked by a portico above. Between the two wings is a basin with bas reliefs and statues around it. Three large bronze statues by Bourdelle represent **France, Strength** and **Victory.** In the programme for the restructurization of French museums, this building will hold the **Maison de l'Image,** a huge collection of everything to do with cinema and photography.

MUSEUM OF MODERN ART OF THE CITY OF PARIS – This museum's collections of paintings serve to recall the importance which the Parisian school had in the development of painting in the 20th century. It contains paintings by Modigliani, Rouault, Utrillo, Picasso, Dufy, Vlaminck, Derain and others, and sculpture by Zadkin, Maillol and others. The largest picture in the world is also exhibited here: the *Fée Electricité,* by Dufy, with an area of nearly 6500 square feet.

From here we move on to **Place du Trocadéro,** the name of which derives from a Spanish fortress which the French conquered in 1823. In the centre is the equestrian **statue** of Marshal Foch (R. Wlérick and R. Martin, 1951). At the corner of Avenue Georges-Mandel is the wall of the **Passy Cemetery**. In it are buried a number of great men: the painters Manet and Berthe Morisot, the writers Giraudoux and Tristan Bernard and the composers Debussy and Fauré. Las Cases, the companion of Napoleon during his exile on St Helena, is also buried here.

This area is the quarter of Passy, known in the past for its ferruginous waters. In Rue Franklin, at no. 8, is the **Clemenceau Museum,** occupying the apartment of the great statesman (known as the "Tiger"), which has been kept exactly as it was on the day of his death in 1929 and which contains documents and souvenirs of his long career as a journalist and politician.

At no. 47 Rue Raynouard is the house inhabited by Balzac from 1840 to 1847, now a museum containing various objects which belonged to the great writer. Finally, continuing along this street as far as Place du Docteur-Hayem, we reach the **Maison de Radio-France,** headquarters of the French Radio and Television, built between 1959 and 1964 by H. Bernard with a tower 230 feet high, 1000 offices, 62 studios and five auditoriums.

PALAIS DE CHAILLOT

Along with the gardens of the Trocadéro, the Champs-Élysées and the Eiffel Tower, the Palais de Chaillot constitutes a fine example of the architecture at the beginning of the 20th century. It was built for the Exhibition held in Paris in 1937. Its architects were Boileau, Azéma and Carlu, who planned the present building on the site of another previous structure, the Trocadéro. Of the latter, built by Napoleon for his son, the King of Rome, only the plans by Percier and Fontaine remain. The Chaillot Palace consists of two enormous pavilions which stretch out in two wings, united by a central terrace with statues of gilt bronze. From here a vast and splendid complex of terraces and stairways, embellished with fountains and jets of water, slopes down to the Seine. The two pavilions, on the front of which are engraved verses by the poet Valéry, today contain the Museum of the Navy, the Museum of Man and the Museum of French Monuments.

MUSEUM OF THE NAVY – This is one of the richest museums of its type in the world. It contains models of ships, original objects, souvenirs and works of art linked to the sea. Among these are the models of Columbus' ship, the Santa Maria, and the ship **La Belle Poule,** which brought back to France the ashes of Napoleon from St Helena.

MUSEUM OF MAN – This contains important collections of anthropology and ethnology, illustrating the various human races and their ways of life. In the gallery of paleontology, there are some very famous prehistoric discoveries: the **Venus of Lespugue,** made from mammoth's ivory, a cast of the **Hottentot Venus** and the **Hoggar frescoes.** Particularly rich are the collections from the American continent, including Pre-Columbian, Maya, Aztec and Toltec art. From Asia there are Siberian, Mongolian, Chinese, Tibetan and Indochinese objects, besides evidence of the civilisations of Polynesia, the Easter Islands, Java and Malaysia.

MUSEUM OF THE FRENCH MONUMENTS – Born in 1880 from an idea of Viollet-le-Duc, it offers a vast artistic panorama from the Carolingian period on. The works are grouped according to regions, schools and periods, so that the visitor can study the evolution, characteristics and influence of each style. In the sculpture section, the works include Romanesque, Gothic (statues from the cathedrals of Chartres, Amiens, Notre-Dame and Rheims), Renaissance (works by Jean Goujon and Germain Pilon) and modern (Rude, Pigalle, Houdon).

Also in the complex of the Palais de Chaillot is the **Théâtre de Chaillot,** situated below the terrace, with a capacity of 3000 persons. In 1948 and in 1951-1952 it was used for the third and fourth sessions of the General Assembly of the United Nations.

In a grotto in the garden is the **Aquarium,** in which the life of most of the freshwater fishes from all over France can be observed. The gardens slope gently down to the Seine, which the **Pont d'Iéna** (1813) crosses here. Adorned with four equestrian groups at the ends, the bridge links Place de Varsovie to the other bank, dominated by the Eiffel Tower.

EIFFEL TOWER

The Eiffel Tower, which has become the symbol of Paris, was erected for the World Fair in 1889. A masterpiece designed by the engineer Gustave Eiffel, it is altogether 1050 feet high, an extremely light, interlaced structure made of 15,000 pieces of metal welded together. Its weight of 7000 tons rests on four huge piers with cement bases. It has three floors: the first at 187 feet, the second at 337 and the third at 899. Bars and restaurants on the first two allow the tourist

Eiffel Tower.

Three evocative pictures of the Eiffel Tower.

to pause and enjoy the astonishing view and splendid land-scape. On days of perfect visibility, the eye can see almost 45 miles.

CHAMP-DE-MARS

This carpet of green stretching beneath the Eiffel Tower was originally a military parade ground, but was later transformed into a garden. During the Ancien Régime and the Revolution, many festivals were held there, including the famous Festival of the Supreme Being, introduced by Robespierre and celebrated on 8 June 1794. In modern times, the area has been the site of numerous World Fairs. Today the garden, the design of which was supervised by Formigé between 1908 and 1928, is divided by wide paths and embellished by small lakes, watercourses and flower beds.

MILITARY ACADEMY

The École Militaire, the French Military Academy, stands at the end of the panoramic Champ-de-Mars. Built on the initiative of the financier Pâris-Duverney and of Madame Pompadour, who wanted young men of the poorer classes to be able to take up military careers, it was constructed between 1751 and 1773 by the architect Jacques-Ange Gabriel. The façade has two orders of windows and in the centre is a pavilion with columns which support the pediment, decorated with statues and covered by a cupola. The grace-ful **Courtyard of Honour** has a portico of twin Doric columns and the façade is formed by three pavilions linked by two rows of columns. Still in use as a military academy today, it was entered in 1784 by Napoleon Bonaparte, who left the following year with the rank of second lieutenant in the artillery.

MAISON DE L'U.N.E.S.C.O. – Standing behind the Military Academy, it was constructed in 1955-1958 by three great modern architects: the American Breuer, the Italian Nervi and the Frenchman Zehrfuss. They planned it as a Y-shaped building, with large windows and curving front. Great artists collaborated in the decoration and embellishment of the vast complex, among them Henry Moore, Calder, Miro, Jean Arp, Picasso and Le Corbusier.

LES INVALIDES

Stretching between Place Vauban and the Esplanade des Invalides, this vast complex of buildings includes the Hôtel des Invalides, the Dôme and the church of St-Louis.
The whole construction, which Louis XIV ordered built and the commission for which was given to Libéral Bruant in 1671, was designed as a refuge for old and invalid soldiers, who were then often forced to beg for a living. The vast square of the Esplanade (1704-1720) is 520 yards long and

View of the Champ de Mars from above
and the façade of the École Militaire.

270 yards wide, creating perfect surroundings for the **Hôtel**. In the garden in front of the Hôtel bronze cannon of the 17th and 18th century are lined up, eighteen pieces belonging to the "triumphal battery", which were fired only on important occasions. The façade, 643 feet long, has four ordes of windows and a majestic portal in the centre, surmounted by a relief representing *Louis XIV* with *Prudence* and *Justice* at his sides. In the courtyard, the four sides consist of two levels of arcades, and the pavilion at the end becomes the façade of the church of St-Louis. In the centre is the *statue* by Seurre depicting Napoleon (previously on top of the Vendôme Column). The **church of St-Louis-des-Invalides,** designed by Hardouin-Mansart, has three aisles. Many flags hang from its walls. In the crypt Rouget de Lisle, author of the Marseillaise, is buried together with the Marshals of France and Governors des Invalides.

MUSEUM OF THE ARMY – This museum, the richest military museum in the world, is housed in the buildings beside the Hôtel's main courtyard. Besides arms and armour from the 14th century to our own times there are also historical relics and souvenirs of great importance and value. In some of the cases are the flagstaffs of the flags burnt after the fall of Napoleon, the farewell flag flown by the Emperor at Fontainebleau, the cannonball which killed Turenne and the wooden leg of General Daumesnil. From this often moving display, we can pass on to the **Museum of Relief Maps and Plans,** which contains models and relief maps of the cities, harbours and strongholds of France and Europe.

DÔME DES INVALIDES

The Dôme, with its entrance in Place Vauban, is the real masterpiece of Hardouin-Mansart, who built it between 1679 and 1706. It has a square plan and two orders. The façade above all is a work of elegance and symmetry: above the two orders of columns surmounted by a pediment is the solid mass of the drum with its twin columns. Soaring above this, after a sober series of corbels, is the slim cupola, decorated with garlands and floral motifs. Covered with gilt leaves, the cupola terminates in a small lantern with spire, 350 feet above ground level.

Interior. In the form of a Greek cross, it is as simple as the exterior. The *four Evangelists* painted in the pendentives of the cupola are by Charles de la Fosse, who also painted the large figure of *St Louis presenting Christ with his Sword.* The church contains the tombs of some members of the Bonaparte family and other great men of France. In the chapels on the right are the *tombs of Joseph Bonaparte,* and, more northwards, those of Marshals Foch and Vauban, in the first chapel on the left the tomb of Napoleon's other brother, Jerome, followed by the tombs of Turenne and Lyautey.

Dôme des Invalides.

Tomb of Napoleon I.

TOMB OF NAPOLEON – It is in a crypt exactly below the centre of the cupola. The Emperor, who died on St Helena on 5 May 1821, was not brought back to Paris until 1840; in that year, on 15 December, his body was interred here in a ceremony of unequalled solemnity. The body is enclosed in six coffins: the first of tin sheeted iron, the second of mahogany, the third and fourth of lead, the fifth of ebony and the sixth of oak. These were then placed in the great red porphyry sarcophagus in the crypt designed by Visconti. Here 12 enormous *Victories* by Pradier keep a vigil over the Emperor. Next to him is the tomb of his son, "l'Aiglon" (the Eaglet), who died in Vienna in 1832.

RODIN MUSEUM – With its entrance in Rue de Varenne no. 77, the Rodin Museum is in the **Hôtel Biron,** constructed in 1728-1731 by Gabriel and Aubert and the property of Marshal de Biron. In 1820 the building became a convent of the Sacred Heart nuns, where the daughters of the great French families were educated. The Neo-Gothic church erected in the courtyard, under the Mother Superior Sophie Barat, belongs to this period. In 1904 the building was rented to the Victor Duruy secondary school, and later it was put at the disposal of the sculptor Auguste Rodin, who on his death in 1917 left his works to the State. The museum contains a splendid collection of the great sculptor's works. It has about 500 pieces of sculpture, in bronze and white marble. Among the many, we should mention the *Burgher of Calais,* the *Thinker* and the *statue of Balzac* in the main courtyard, the *Count Ugolino group* in the garden, the *Kiss* and the *St John the Baptist* in the hall on the ground floor.

FROM THE PALAIS BOURBON *(Métro: line 12 – Chambre des Députés station)* **TO MONTPARNASSE.**

Palais Bourbon – Palais de la Légion d'Honneur **– Institute of France** – The Mint – Place St-Germain-des-Prés *–* **St-Germain-des-Prés –** **St-Sulpice** – Les Carmes **– Luxembourg** – Petit Luxembourg – Avenue de l'Observatoire – Observatory – Catacombs – Montparnasse – Cemetery – Bourdelle Museum – Pasteur Institute.

Faubourg St-Germain – This Left Bank quarter, a suburb built around the church of St-Germain-des-Prés, is in some respects the aristocratic quarter of Paris: here wealthy burghers, financiers and aristocrats from Marais built their elegant dwellings, with splendid courtyards and vast gardens. These luxurious residences were eventually occupied by embassies and ministries. The decline of the area began under Louis-Philippe and Napoleon III, when the Champs-Elysées gradually took the place of St-Germain.

PALAIS BOURBON

This palace is in front of the Pont de la Concorde (1790), creating a symmetrical relationship with the Madeleine. Today it is the seat of the National Assembly. It is the work of four architects: Giardini began it in 1722, Lassurance continued its construction, and Aubert and Gabriel completed it in 1728. It was originally built for the daughter of Louis XIV, the Duchess of Bourbon, who gave her name to the palace. In 1764 it became the property of the Prince of Condé and was

Palais Bourbon.

extended to its present dimensions. Napoleon had the façade built by Poyet between 1803 and 1807. On the portico is an allegorical pediment (Cortot, 1842). The other allegorical bas reliefs on the wings are by Rude and Pradier.

Interior. It contains a wealth of works of art. Between 1838 and 1845 Delacroix decorated the **Library** with paintings illustrating the *History of Civilisation*. Also in the Library are *busts of Diderot and Voltaire,* sculpted by Houdon.

We now walk along the typical Rue de Lille which, along with Rue de Varenne, Rue Grenelle and Rue de l'Université, still preserves the spirit of the Faubourg St-Germain of former times.

PALAIS DE LA LEGION D'HONNEUR — In Rue de Lille no. 64, this building was constructed by the architect Rousseau in 1787 for the Prince de Salm and burnt down in 1871 during the period of the Commune; it was rebuilt in its original form in 1878. Headquarters since 1804 of the order of the Legion of Honour (instituted by Napoleon in 1802), it has a majestic portal and a colonnaded courtyard. The building contains the **Museum of the Legion of Honour,** containing many relics and documents related to the order created by Napoleon and other European orders of chivalry.
Alongside this building is the **Gare d'Orsay,** a railway station built in 1900 but today almost completely in disuse. Continuing along the Seine, we reach the picturesque bridge, the **Pont des Arts,** in front of the Louvre: it is the city's first iron bridge, and is now open only to pedestrians.

INSTITUTE OF FRANCE

The building was erected in 1665 as the result of a legacy left by Cardinal Mazarin who in 1661, three days before his death, left 2 million livres for the construction of a college to accommodate 60 scholars and to be called the College of the Four Nations. Napoleon in 1806 transferred here the Institute of France, which had been formed in 1795 by the amalgamation of five academies: the Academy of France and the Academies of Science, Belles Lettres, Fine Arts and Political Sciences. The building was designed by the architect Le Vau, who took his inspiration from the Baroque buildings of Rome. It consists of a central body with a colonnaded façade, the columns supporting a pediment above which is a fine cupola (on the drum are engraved the insignia of Mazarin). This part is linked to the lateral pavilions by two curving wings, with two orders of pillars. Entering the courtyard we find on the left the **Mazarin Library** and on the right the **Ceremonial Hall.** Here, below the cupola in what was originally the college chapel, the solemn ceremony for the presentation of new members of the French Academy takes place. The vestibule preceding the hall contains the *Tomb of Mazarin* (Coysevox, 1689).

THE MINT — The Mint (La Monnaie) is at no. 11 Quai de Conti, next to the Institute. Its imposing building was constructed in 1771-1777 by the architect Antoine. The facade, more than 380 feet long, is simple in line, with three orders of windows and a projecting central body with colonnade. Inside, a monumental stairway leads up to the **Museum of the Mint,** with its collections of coins and medals ancient and modern.

Pont des Arts and Institute of France in the background.

The Seine seen from Pont des Arts.

PLACE ST-GERMAIN-DES-PRÉS – Passing through the tiny streets typical of this quarter, full of antiquarians and art merchants, we reach this square, the heart of old Paris and a meeting place for the Left Bank intellectuals. In the narrow streets of this quarter are the cellars where the Existentialist movement was born. Two cafés in the square, the *Café de Flore* and the *Café des Deux Magots,* saw the birth of this movement, while in the tavern called the *Brasserie Lipp* Paul Valéry, Max Jacob, Leon Blum and J. Giraudoux used to meet and talk.

ST-GERMAIN-DES-PRÉS

A rare example of Romanesque architecture in Paris, St-Germain is the city's oldest church. It was erected in the 11th and 12th centuries, and though devastated no less than four times in forty years by the Normans it was rebuilt each time in its severe Romanesque forms. In front of it are the remains of the 12th-century portal, half-hidden by the 17th-century porch which was erected in 1607. The bell tower, on the other hand, is completely Romanesque, with its corners strengthened by robust buttresses.

Interior. It has three aisles and a transept, the end of which was modified in the 17th century. The chancel and ambulatory still retain much of the original 12th-century architecture. In the second chapel on the right is the *tomb of the great philosopher Descartes,* and in the left transept is that of the Polish king *John Casimir.*

On the left side of the church, in front of Rue de l'Abbaye, is the tiny Rue de Furstenberg: at no. 6 is the house where Eugene Delacroix died in 1863. Today the house contains the painter's personal effects. Not far from St-Germain, in a quarter where there are many shops selling religious objects and sacred images, is Place St-Sulpice, with the church of the same name.

ST-SULPICE

St-Sulpice is the largest church in Paris after Notre-Dame. Six architects directed its construction over a period of 134 years. The last of these, the Florentine G. N. Servandoni, erected the imposing façade, though it was later partly modified by Maclaurin and Chalgrin. Today it cor sists of a double portico surmounted by a loggia with balcony and flanked by two towers. The façades of the transept at the sides of the church have two orders, one above the other, in the Jesuit style.

Interior. It is impressive and grandiose: 361 feet long, 182 feet wide and 108 feet high (thus larger than, but not so high as St-Eustache). Above the entrance is one of the finest organs in France, designed by Chalgrin in 1776 and reconstructed in 1862 by Cavaillé-Coll. The two *holywater stoups* against the first pillars of the nave are giant shells given to François I by the Republic of Venice and donated to the church by Louis XV in 1745. The splendid frescoes in the first chapel on the right, full of Romantic vigour, were painted by Eugene Delacroix between 1849 and 1861. On the right wall, *Heliodorus being driven from the Temple,*

SAINT-GERMAIN-DES-PRES – **Exterior**.

on the left, *Jacob struggling with the Angel,* and in the vault, *St Michael killing the Dragon.* There are two statues by Bouchardon, *Our Lady of the Sorrows* and *Christ against the Pillar,* on the pillars in the chancel. In the Lady Chapel, decoration of which was supervised by Servandoni, there is a *Virgin and Child* by Pigalle in the niche above the altar, plus canvases by Van Loo on the walls and a fresco by Lemoyne in the dome.

LES CARMES — At no. 70 Rue de Vaugirard, this is the ancient monastery of the Barefoot Carmelites, founded in 1611. It is an infamous site, because here, on 2 September 1792, 115 monks were massacred without pity, guilty of not have taken the oath specified by the Civil Constitution for the Clergy. The tomb of the victims is in the crypt.

LUXEMBOURG

Rue de Vaugirard takes us directly to the main point of interest in this quarter, the Luxembourg Palace, surrounded by its famous garden.

PALACE — Its construction was due to Marie de' Medici who, after the death of King Henri IV, decided to live not in the Louvre but in a place which in some way reminded her of Florence, the city from which she came. In 1612 she acquired the mansion of Duke François of Luxembourg, with its extensive grounds, and in 1615 commissioned Salomon de Brosse to erect a palace, the style and materials of which were to be as similar as possible to those of the Florentine palaces which she had left to come to France. And in fact the building's rustication and large ringed columns recall the Palazzo Pitti in Florence more than any other palace in Paris. The façade consists of a pavilion with two orders covered by a cupola, with two wings at the sides linked to the central building by galleries. When the Revolution broke out, the palace was taken from the royal family and converted into a State prison. On 4 November 1795 the First Directory adopted it as its seat, and Napoleon later used it as the Senate's chambers. To visit the interior of the palace, permission from the Secretary-General of the Senate is needed. The Library is decorated with celebrated pictures by Delacroix *(Dante and*

LUXEMBOURG: **The Palace.**

LUXEMBOURG GARDEN – **The Medici Fountain.**

Virgil in Limbo, Alexander puts Homer's Poems in the Casket of Darius), painted in 1847, and on the ceiling of the Gallery are the Signs of the Zodiac, painted by Jordaens.

GARDENS – Covering no less than 57 acres, the gardens are a public park frequented every day by students from the Latin Quarter. Among the trees one can find fountains, groups of statues and even playing fields. A fine series of statues depicting the queens of France and illustrious women lines the terraces of the park. At the end of a canal on the eastern side of the palace, framed by the greenery, is the splendid **Medici Fountain,** attributed to Salomon de Brosse. In the central niche is depicted *Polyphemus surprising Galatea with the shepherd Acis,* by Ottin, 1863. On the back is a bas relief of *Leda and the Swan* done by Valois in 1806.

The Fountain of the Four Parts of the World.

PETIT LUXEMBOURG — This is on the right of the Luxembourg Palace, with its entrance at no. 17 Rue de Vaugirard. Once the property of Marie de' Medici and of Cardinal Richelieu, it is now occupied by the president of the Senate.

AVENUE DE L'OBSERVATOIRE — This is a splendid avenue lined with trees, which runs from the Luxembourg Gardens to the Observatory. In the middle of the avenue, surrounded by greenery, is the celebrated fountain called the *Fountain of the Four Parts of the World* (Davioud, 1875). It has a group of maidens who symbolise the four parts of the world, sculpted with extraordinary lightness and grace by Carpeaux.

OBSERVATORY — At the end of the avenue is the Observatory, seat of the International Time Bureau since 1919. Construction of the Observatory, designed by Claude Perrault, was begun by order of Colbert on 21 June 1667 (the day of the summer solstice). The four walls of the building are oriented exactly to the four cardinal points of the compass, and the Paris meridian of longitude passes exactly through the building's centre.

From here one reaches **Place Denfert-Rochereau,** the square which takes its name from the colonel who fiercely opposed the Germans at Belfort in 1870. Here too is the entrance to the **Catacombs,** limestone quarries of the Gallo-Roman era which were used as ossuaries in 1785. Here thousands upon thousands of bones, brought from many cemeteries in the city, were placed. It is very probable that the skeletons include the remains (though no longer identifiable) of many protagonists of the Revolution (Robespierre, Danton, St Just), thrown into common graves.

MONTPARNASSE

The name Montparnasse derives from a small hill familiarly called Mount Parnassus which was levelled during the 18th century. During the years between 1920 and 1940, the quarter was frequented above all by artists, writers and painters, who gave Montparnasse its typically Bohemian atmosphere, making it the companion and rival of the other celebrated quarter of Montmartre. The nerve centre of the area is **Carrefour Raspail,** the crossroads where Boulevard Raspail and Boulevard Montparnasse meet. Here stands one of Rodin's finest works, the bronze representing *Balzac,* 9 ft 2 in high, done in 1897.

CEMETERY — This is one of the most interesting places in the area to visit. Built in 1824, in it are buried writers (Proudhon, Maupassant, Huysmans, Baudelaire), painters (Fantin-Latour, Soutine), sculptors (Brancusi, Rude, Houdon, Tristan Tzara), composers (Franck, Saint-Saens) and Captain Dreyfus, protagonist and victim of the famous "Dreyfus Affair".
Despite the many building constructions which have changed the quarter's appearance, making it much more modern, Montparnasse nevertheless preserves many signs of its artistically rich past. At no. 16 Rue Bourdelle is the **Bourdelle Museum,** which contains almost all the works done by the sculptor Antoine Bourdelle (sculpture, paintings, drawings). In the scientific field, the quarter has the **Pasteur Institute,** with laboratories and facilities for research, a centre which makes serums and vaccines and a very well equipped hospital. In this building is the crypt where the great doctor Pasteur himself is buried.

Montparnasse also contains a rare example of the technique of metal construction applied to a religious building: the church of **Notre-Dame du Travail,** built in 1900. Further on, we come to **Rue de la Gaîté,** so called because in the 18th century it was lined by restaurants, cabarets and dance halls. At no. 20 today is the **Bobino,** a famous music hall.

Montparnasse.

ITINERARY 7

VISIT TO THE LATIN QUARTER - FROM ST-SÉVERIN *(Métro: line 4 – St-Michel station)* **TO ST-NICOLAS-DU-CHARDONNET.**

Boulevard St-Michel – **St-Séverin** – St-Julien-le-Pauvre – Square René Viviani – **Hôtel de Cluny** – École de Médecine – Collège de France – **Sorbonne** – **Panthéon** – Lycée Henri IV – **St-Etienne-du-Mont** – St-Jacques-du-Haut-Pas – **Val-de-Grâce** – St-Medard – Gobelins Tapestry Factory – Place d'Italie – Salpêtrière Hospital – **Jardin des Plantes** – Mosque – Arènes de Lutèce – St-Nicolas-du-Chardonnet.

LATIN QUARTER

The Latin Quarter has become synonymous with the Sorbonne University. An extremely old part of Paris, it became its scholarly centre in the 13th century when the University was moved from the Ile-de-la-Cité to the Left Bank. The University quickly gained fame because students were attracted by the great masters who taught there (St Bonaventura, St Thomas Aquinas, St Albert the Great). Our itinerary through the Latin Quarter can begin from **Place St-Michel,** dating from the time of Napoleon III. Its fine **fountain** (Davioud, 1860) is adorned by the bronze group of St Michael defeating the Dragon. In this square, in August 1944, bitter fighting took place between the students of the Resistance and the Germans.

BOULEVARD ST-MICHEL – This wide avenue, built during the Second Empire and familiarly called by the Parisians "Boul' Mich", ascends from the Seine towards the hill of Ste Geneviève. Animated by its new and second-hand bookshops, noisy cafés, exotic restaurants and avant-garde cinemas, it is the heart of the quarter.

ST-SÉVERIN

From as early as the end of the 11th century, St-Séverin was the parish church of the whole Left Bank. Its construction as it stands today was begun in the first half of the 13th century and lasted until the end of the 16th. Here, legend relates, Dante came to pray at the time of his hypothetical trip to Paris, perhaps in 1307. The **west door,** dating from the 13th century, comes from the church of St-Pierre-aux-Boeufs, demolished in 1839. The windows and rose window above it are in the Flamboyant Gothic style of the 15th century, while the bell tower standing on the left is from the 13th century. Small sculpted cusps run along the sides and around the apse of the church.

Interior. It is 164 feet long, 112 feet wide and 56 feet high, with five aisles, no transept and a small chancel. The first three bays of the nave are the oldest, belonging to the 13th century, while the others date from the 15th and 16th centuries. Above the arcades is the triforium gallery, the oldest in Paris. In the first bays, the pillars are adorned with capitals, unlike those of the following bays, which are in the Flamboyant Gothic style. The **apse** has five arcades which are higher than those in the chancel. Admirable in the chancel is the splendid double ambulatory, erected between 1489 and 1494, with its multiple rib tracery radiating out from the top of the columns. The windows have beautiful stained glass from the end of the 15th century. The stained-glass window in the façade illustrates the *Tree of Jesse* (early 16th century).

ST-JULIEN-LE-PAUVRE — Although small, this church is extremely picturesque. It is one of the oldest churches in Paris, its construction dating back to the same period as that of Notre-Dame (from about 1165 to 1220). Since 1889 it has been a Catholic church of the Malachite rite. The structure of the church was considerably modified in the 17th century, when two bays of the nave and the facade were demolished.

Interior. It has three aisles, pillars with fine capitals carved with acanthus leaves, and three apses.

RENÉ VIVIANI SQUARE — This small square planted with lime-trees stands in front of the church. Here, in 1683, a Robinia tree was planted: introduced from North American by the botanist Robin, from whom it took its name, the tree is now one of the oldest in Paris. The view of the side of Notre-Dame from here is perhaps the finest in the city.

HÔTEL DE CLUNY

This building, standing in its green garden, is without doubt one of the finest examples of Flamboyant Gothic architecture. The Hôtel stands on the site of the ruins of the Roman baths, dating from the 2nd or early 3rd century. The site was the property of the Abbey of Cluny in Burgundy and on it, between 1485 and 1498, Abbot Jacques d'Amboise had a building constructed to accommodate the Benedictine monks who came from Cluny to visit the capital. During the Revolution it became the property of the State and was sold, becoming in 1833 the residence of the collector Alexandre du Sommerard. On his death in 1842, both the building and the collections which it contained passed to the State. In 1844 the museum was opened; it contains objects which illustrate the life of medieval France, including costumes, arms, goldsmiths' works, ceramics, tapestries, paintings and statues.

MUSEUM

Entrance to the Museum is from the courtyard. From here the whole building can be admired in all its beauty: it has two orders of cross windows and a tower containing a staircase, ornamented with the emblems of St James. The balustrade on the roof and the dormer windows are typical of the Flamboyant Gothic style.

The Museum consists of 24 rooms. One of its most precious collections is the one of tapestries woven in the Loire and in Flanders in the 15th and 16th centuries. Room XI, also called the Rotunda, contains the famous series of tapestries of the *Lady and the Unicorn,* from the early 16th century.

A beautiful view of the Pantheon.

THE MUSEUM OF CLUNY – **The gothic ribbing of the vault in the Chapel.**

On this floor, the most famous room is without doubt Room XX, the **Chapel,** the ancient oratory of the abbots. In pure Flamboyant Gothic style, it has a single pillar in the centre, from which the ribs of the vault fan out; along the walls is a series of niches standing on consoles containing the statues of the d'Amboise family. In this chapel are the celebrated tapestries illustrating the *Legend of St Stephen,* woven for the cathedral of Auxerre and completed towards 1490. In the next room is another great tapestry from the beginning of the 16th century depicting the *Parable of the Prodigal Son.*

ÉCOLE DE MÉDECINE – The School of Medicine, at no. 12 in the pictur-esque Rue de l'École de Médecine, was constructed between 1769 and 1786. Its enlargement in 1878-1900 led to the demolition of historic buildings, including the house where Charlotte Corday stabbed Marat to death and the studio where Courbet worked. In front of the building is a *statue of Danton* (A. Paris, 1891).

COLLÈGE DE FRANCE – Standing on the remains of Gallo-Roman baths, it was constructed between 1610 and 1778 by Chalgrin. The Collège de France was created in 1530 by François I as a place of learning independent from the Sorbonne. Since 1852 it has been dependent on the Ministry for National Education, but independent courses of literature and scientific subjects are given here. In front of it is a garden in which are a *statue of Dante* (Aubé, 1879) and a monument representing the *Pléiade*. In an underground laboratory is the cyclotron, with which Frédéric Jolio-Curie achieved the fission of the uranium nucleus.

Church of the Sorbonne.

SORBONNE

The name Sorbonne is used to indicate the complex of buildings which the University of Paris has occupied for seven centuries. In 1253 the confessor of King Louis IX, Robert de Sorbon, founded a college in which theology was also taught to poorer students, and this was the original nucleus of what was to be the famous university. In the vast area which it occupies today are the various institutes and lecture rooms besides other parts such as the library and the chancellor's lodge.

CHURCH OF THE SORBONNE

This is the oldest part of the university's buildings; erected between 1635 and 1642 by Lemercier, it has a typically Baroque façade with two orders, surmounted and dominated by its elegant cupola. Volutes link the lower order to the upper. The columns at ground level become flatter pilaster strips higher up, thus creating a gradual concentration of the luminous quality of the structure.

Interior. In the transept is the white marble *tomb of Cardinal Richelieu,* sculpted by Girardon to a design by Le Brun in 1694.

The hill on which we are now is called the Montagne Ste Geneviève. We walk along Rue Soufflot, full of bookshops and publishers of legal works. At the top of the street, at the corner of Place du Panthéon, are on the left the **Faculty of Law** (Soufflot, 1770) and on the right the **Town Hall of the 5th Arrondissement** (Hittorf, 1850). In the square, which is dominated by the majestic mass of the Panthéon, is the **Library of Ste Geneviève,** designed by Labrouste (1844-1850), with a wealth of manuscripts and early printed books. At the sides of the Panthéon are two marble statues, representing *Corneille* and *Rousseau.*

PANTHÉON

Born as the church of Ste Geneviève because of a vow made in 1744 by Louis XV when he was seriously ill, the Panthéon was designed by Soufflot in 1758 and completed unter the supervision of Rondelet in 1789. During the Revolution, it became the Temple of Fame, in which the nation's great men were buried. Napoleon reopened it for worship in 1806, but this lasted only until 1885 when it reverted once and for all to its status as a secular temple. Its dimensions are exceptional: 360 feet long by 272 feet high. A stairway in front of the temple leads up to a pronaos with 22 columns, supporting a pediment on which in 1831 David d'Angers sculpted the allegorical work representing the *Nation between Liberty and History.* Here can also be read the celebrated inscription: "Aux grandes hommes, la patrie reconnaissante" ("To the great men, from their grateful fatherland"). The great dome dominates the whole building, its drum surrounded by a portico of Corinthian columns.

Rue Soufflot and the Panthéon.

Interior. In the form of a Greek cross, with the dome above the crossing, supported by four pillars, on one of which is the *tomb of Rousseau.* On the walls are *Stories of St Geneviève,* painted by Puvis de Chavannes. Below the temple is the crypt, containing the remains of many great men. Among the many are those of Victor Hugo (transferred here in 1885), Emile Zola, Voltaire, Carnot, Mirabeau and the designer of the building himself, Soufflot.

There are 425 steps leading up to the **dome,** from which there is a vast and impressive panoramic view.

LYCÉE HENRI-IV — Behind the Panthéon, this is where King Clovis, after his victory over the Visigoths at Vouillé, had a basilica constructed in 510 to

ST-ÉTIENNE-DU-MONT — Façade.

contain the remains of his wife Clotilda and of St Geneviève. All that remain of this building are the refectory and the bell-tower of the church, called the **Tower of Clovis,** in Romanesque and Gothic styles. The secondary school called the Lycée Henri-IV has occupied the since 1796.

ST-ÉTIENNE-DU-MONT

This is one of the most unusual churches in Paris, because of both its façade and the interior. It was begun in 1492 but completed only in 1622. The façade is a bizarre amalgamation of Gothic and Renaissance styles, with three superimposed pediments.

Interior. The inside is also extremely unusual. In Gothic

ST-ÉTIENNE-DU-MONT – **Interior and roodscreen.**

style with three aisles and transept, it has very high cylindrical piers supporting the vaulting, linked by a tribune running above the arcades. But the most interesting part of the church is the **jubé,** the roodscreen which separates the nave from the chancel. It was possibly designed by Philibert Delorme and is the only existing roodscreen known in Paris; it was erected between 1521 and 1545. Its rich openwork of Renaissance inspiration continues in the two spiral staircases at the sides. In the ambulatory, alongside the pillars of the Lady Chapel, are the *tombs of Pascal and of Racine.* The church also has fine stained glass from the 16th and 17th centuries.

St-Etienne also contains the *shrine of St Geneviève,* patron saint of Paris, who in 451 saved the city from the menace of the Huns.

Along **Rue St Jacques,** one of the oldest and most important streets on the Left Bank, we find the **church of St-Jacques-du-Haut-Pas** (1630-1685), one of the most fervid centres of the Jansenist movement.

VAL-DE-GRÂCE

Construction of this splendid architectural complex in the 17th century was due to Anne of Austria, who at the age of 38 had not yet had any children and made a vow to construct a magnificent church if she should finally give birth to an heir. In 1638 the future Louis XIV was born, and work on the church was begun immediately to the plans prepared by François Mansart. In 1645 the young king himself laid the foundation stone. But the queen decided that Mansart was too slow and appointed Le Mercier to take his place. Yet another architect, Le Duc, completed the church in 1667. It was consecrated in 1710. Constructed in the Jesuit style, Val-de-Grâce has a façade with two orders of columns and double superimposed triangular pediments. Above these in turn is the beautiful, slender cupola, 131 feet high.

Interior. The interior is in the purest Baroque style: without aisles, with barrel vaulting, linking chapels on the sides and a chancel with six chapels (two on the sides and four in the corners). The cupola is adorned by a grandiose fresco by P. Mignard, depicting the *Glory of the Elect,* in which there are over 200 figures, three times larger than lifesize. The sculptural decoration is the work of Anguier and Philippe Buyster. On the right is the **St Louis Chapel,** the former chancel of the Benedictines; on the left, the **St Anne Chapel,** in which from 1662 the hearts of the royal and Orléans families were placed, though they disappeared in 1792 during the Revolution. Of the former Benedictine monastery which stood here, the fine **cloister** with its two orders of galleries and the pavilion where Anne of Austria stayed can still be seen today.

ST-MEDARD – The church stands at the end of Rue Mongue, in front of the colourful and lively Rue Mouffetard. Dedicated to St Medard, the counsellor of the Merovingian kings, it was begun in the 15th century and not completed until 1655. In the **façade** is a great Flamboyant Gothic window; the nave inside is in the same style, while the chancel is in the Renaissance style. The church contains some interesting works of art: a painting attributed to Zurbaran, depicting *St Joseph and the Christ Child,* in the third chapel on the right, and a *Dead Christ,* possibly by Philippe de Champaigne, in the second chapel on the right in the chancel.

GOBELINS' TAPESTRY FACTORY – The Gobelins' tapestry factory, famous throughout the world, is at no. 42 Avenue des Gobelins. A dyer called Jean Gobelin set up his small workshop in this building in 1440. In 1601 it was sold by his descendants to two Flemish tapestry workers, summoned to Paris from Brussels by King Henri IV. Then in 1662 Louis XIV ordered Colbert to group the city's various dying shops together here, thus creating the "Royal

Factory of Tapestry Makers to the Crown", to which five years later the Royal Cabinet-Makers were added. More than 5000 tapestries of great value have been woven here to the cartoons of the great masters (Poussin, Van Loo, Boucher and even Picasso). The craftsmen's methods and organisation in the factory have remained unchanged since the 17th century. Both the workshops and the gallery, where tapestries of the 17th and 18th centuries are exhibited, can be visited.

PLACE D'ITALIE – At the end of Avenue des Gobelins is Place d'Italie, site of the ancient tollhouse of Paris and today the centre of an area in rapid development.

This circular square is where **Boulevard de l'Hôpital** begins, and at no. 47 is the **Salpêtrière Hospital,** the largest hospital complex in Paris. Originally a place where gunpowder was made from saltpetre, it was converted into a hospital by Louis XIV in 1684. In front of the huge and imposing building is a vast Italian garden. In the centre is the octagonal dome of the **St Louis Chapel,** surmounted by a lantern. The interior is original in form: four aisles surrounding a rotunda to form a Greek cross. The young Freud studied in the Salpêtrière Hospital under the guidance of Charcot.

Boulevard de l'Hôpital ends at the **Pont d'Austerlitz** in Place Valhubert, on one side of which is the railway station called the **Gare d'Austerlitz,** built in 1869. In front of the bridge is the main entrance to the Jardin des Plantes.

JARDIN DES PLANTES

The Jardin des Plantes, or Botanical Gardens, dates back to 1626, when Hérouard and Guy de la Brosse, the doctors of Louis XIII, established the Royal Garden of Medicinal Herbs, opened to the public in 1650. Its collections of plants were enriched by Louis XIV's first doctor, Fagon, by the botanist Tournefort, by the three Jussieu brothers, who travelled the world in search of new plants, and above all by the great naturalist Buffon; the latter made the greatest contribution to the gardens, enlarging them as far as the Seine and building the galleries, the maze and the amphitheatre. At the time of the Revolution, the gardens came to house the National Museum of Natural History. As a result of the work of many eminent scholars, this has become one of the richest and most varied museums in the world.

Visit to the gardens. After passing through the gate, we reach the **Botanical garden,** its vast flower beds divided by wide paths. Here are the **School of Botany,** containing more than 10,000 species of plants, all methodically classified; the **Winter Garden,** with tropical plants; the **Alpine Garden,** with collections of plants from the polar regions, the Himalaya Mountains and the Alps.

Museum of Natural History. This is on the other side of the path on the left and contains various sections: *Paleontology* (fossils, prehistoric animals, casts of extinct species), *Botany, Mineralogy* (precious stones, minerals, meteorites) and the *hunting collections of the Duke of Orléans.* In the *Zoology* gallery are important skeletons, shells and stuffed animals. Near this gallery, on the other side of the *Glasshouses* (containing plants from South America, Australia, etc.), is the *Maze,* with its rare plants, including the cedar

The Mosque.

of Lebanon planted in 1734 by Bernard de Jussieu. Also worth visiting is the *Menagerie*, with its wild animals and bird, including elephants, monkeys and so on.

MOSQUE — Near the gardens, with its entrance in Place du Puits-de-l'Ermite, is the Mosque, an unusual corner of the Orient here in the middle of the ancient heart of Paris which cannot fail to attract the tourist's attention. The Mosque has an interesting **courtyard** in Hispano-Moorish style, a **patio** inspired by that of the Alhambra at Granada, and a **prayer chamber** adorned with precious carpets.

ARÈNES DE LUTÈCE (Lutetia Arena) — Its entrance at no. 49 Rue Monge, this is the Roman arena of the ancient city. The exact date of the construction of this Gallo-Roman monument is not known, though it was probably in the 2nd or 3rd century. It was destroyed by the barbarians in 280 and rediscovered only in 1869. At the beginning of this century, it was restored and opened as a park. The arena had the functions of an amphitheatre, where circus games took place, and also of a theatre. The seating section was elliptical in form, with 36 rows of seats, many of which are now lost. The platform on which the stage was and the circular track around the amphitheatre are still visible.

ST-NICOLAS-DU-CHARDONNET — Dedicated to St Nicholas, patron saint of the boatmen, it was built in the Baroque style between 1656 and 1709. On the exterior, the **side door,** carved from wood after a design by Le Brun, is outstanding.

Interior. In Jesuit style, it has three naves with chancel and ambulatory and contains many works of art. In the first chapel on the right, a work by Corot depicting the *Baptism of Jesus;* in the ambulatory, in the second chapel on the right, the *funeral monument to the Solicitor General Jérôme Bignon;* in the second chapel to the left of the apse, the *tomb of the painter Le Brun and his wife,* by Coysevox. Another work by Charles Le Brun, *St Charles Borromeo,* is above the altar.

ITINERARY 8

FROM THE HÔTEL DE VILLE *(Métro: lines 1 and 11 — Hôtel de Ville station)* **TO THE HÔTEL DE SENS.**

Place de l'Hôtel de Ville — **Hôtel de Ville** — **St-Gervais-St-Protais** — Rue des Archives — National Archives — **Palais Soubise** — **Picasso Museum** — **Hôtel de Rohan** — Rue des Francs Bourgeois — **Hôtel Carnavalet** — Musée Carnavalet — **Place des Vosges** — Rue St-Antoine — **St-Paul-St-Louis** — Place de la Bastille — Arsenal Library — **Hôtel de Sens.**

PLACE DE L'HÔTEL DE VILLE — Its present appearance dates from 1853, but for many centuries, from 1310 to 1830, this vast area was the site of public executions (in 1721 the brigand Cartouche was put to death here). Flanked by the Rue de Rivoli on one side and the Seine on the other, it is dominated by the wide façade of the Hôtel de Ville.

HÔTEL DE VILLE

The illustrious old Hôtel de Ville, today the seat of the city's municipal government, stands on the site previously occupied by a 16th-century building designed by Domenico da Cortona and built in the Renaissance style, but destroyed by fire at the time of the Commune in 1871. The present building was inspired by the previous one. Designed by Deperthes and Ballu, it was completed in 1882. It consists of several pavilions surmounted by domes in the form of truncated pyramids, with a forest of statues in every possible angle. There are 136 on the building's four façades, including one on a terrace depicting Etienne Marcel, leader of the Parisian merchants and fomenter of the disorders which crippled Paris in the 14th century. Inside the building, on 27 July 1794, the soldiers of the Convention arrested Robespierre and his followers.

ST-GERVAIS-ST-PROTAIS

Dedicated to St Gervase and St Protase, two brothers martyred under Nero, the church stands on a small square behind the Hôtel de Ville. A Flamboyant Gothic building, it was begun in 1494 and completed in 1657. The **façade** is an imposing example of Classicism (the first in Paris) and was erected between 1616 and 1621 by Métezeau (or by Salomon de Brosse, according to another theory by critics): it has three orders of columns in the Doric, Ionic and Corinthian styles.

Interior. It is divided by pillars into three aisles, with transept, chancel, ambulatory and side chapels. There are fine 16th-century stained-glass windows above the nave and chancel. Above the central door is an organ built in 1601. On the right, in the first chapel, a painting by Sebastiano Ricci;

Hôtel de Ville.

Saint-Gervais – Saint-Protais.

in the ambulatory (fourth chapel on the right), the *tomb of Michel Le Tellier,* chancellor of Louis XIV (Mazeline and Hurtrelle); in the left aisle, in the third chapel, the altar front has a fine stone bas relief of the *Death of the Virgin* (13th century). A little further on is the **Gilded Chapel,** built in 1628, decorated with painted panels inlaid in wood and depicting *Stories of the Life and Passion of Christ.* Against a pillar is a Gothic polychrome stone *Virgin and Child.* Also admirable is the exterior of the apse, with the 17th-century bell-tower.

RUE DES ARCHIVES — This street, running from Rue de Rivoli to the Square du Temple, belonged to the old aristocratic **quarter of Marais,** which became very fashionable at the beginning of the 17th century. In fact this was the birthplace of the typical French *hôtel,* a Classical mansion with garden and courtyard. But when high society moved to the more fashionable areas of Île-St-Louis and later St-Germain, the quarter's decline set in, until it was completely abandoned with the taking of the Bastille. At no. 22 is the **Billettes Church** (1756), and at the following number the only medieval cloister left in Paris can be visited. Further on, at no. 60, is the **Hôtel Guénégaud,** built between 1648 and 1651 by François Mansart and reconstructed in the 18th century: simple and sober in form, it contains the Museum of the Hunt, a collections of arms used in the hunt from prehistoric times down to today.

NATIONAL ARCHIVES — These are the most important buildings in the street and the richest archives in the world: a collection of 6000 million documents related to the history of France from the Merovingian era to our own times. The archives today are contained in the **Palais Soubise** and the **Hôtel de Rohan.**

PALAIS SOUBISE

Entrance to the building is at no. 60 Rue des Francs-Bourgeois: from the courtyard, which has a horseshoe shape, the façade with the *statues of the Seasons* can be admired. On the first floor are the splendid apartments of the Prince and Princess of Soubise, with frescoes by the finest painters and works by the finest sculptors of the era (Boucher, Van Loo, Lemoyne, Adam and others). Here is the **Historical Museum of France,** in which many documents are displayed. Among them are the acts of foundation of the Sainte-Chapelle and the Sorbonne, the Edict of Nantes and its later Revocation, one of the six letters written by Joan of Arc, a glove which belonged to the assassin of the king, Damiens, and the first catalogue of the Louvre Museum, dated 10 August 1793.

THE PICASSO MUSEUM

This recently constituted Museum is situated in Rue de Thorigny in the Hôtel Salé, built in 1656 by J. Boullier for Aubert de Fontenay, a tax collector (hence the building's nickname).
Here "Picasso's Picassos" are exhibited, that is the sculptures and paintings from which the great Spanish artist, who died in 1973, never wanted to be separated: there are over 200 paintings, 158 sculptures, 88 ceramics, over three thousand engravings and sketches and an incredible number of letters,

objects, photographs and manuscripts. Then there is Picasso's personal collection, previously at the Louvre: there are works by Cezanne, Renoir, Braque, Modigliani and Matisse. Amongst the numerous works exhibited there is *Self-Portrait in Blue*, 1901, the *Three Women under a Tree*, painted between 1907 and 1908, the *Great Nude in the Red Armchair*, the *Crucifixion*, 1930 and the *Composition with Butterfly*, 1932, until recently thought to have disappeared. All of these works were given to the French State by the heirs of the Spanish genius as payment for succession duties on the properties owned in France by Picasso.

HÔTEL DE ROHAN

Entrance to the Hôtel is at no. 87 Rue Vieille-du-Temple; the building is linked to the Palais Soubise by a garden, which the main façade overlooks. In the courtyard on the right, above the former stables, are the magnificent *Horses of Apollo*, a masterpiece by Robert Le Lorrain. A stairway leads up to the apartments on the first floor. Among the most interesting parts are the luxurious *Gilded Saloon* and the original *Monkey Room*, decorated by Huet (1749-1752).

RUE DES FRANCS-BOURGEOIS — This is the other important street in this quarter. In 1334 the "maisons d'aumône", or almshouses, were founded here, a place of refuge for poor citizens, who therefore paid no tax, which is what "francs bourgeois" means. Along this street too, which runs from Rue des Archives to Place des Vosges, are the mansions of the aristocrats.

HÔTEL CARNAVALET — **Courtyard and statue of Louis XIV.**

At no. 53 is the back entrance to **Notre-Dame des-Blancs-Manteaux** (a church with a splendid *wooden pulpit* with ivory inlays, a Flemish work done in 1749 in the Rococo style). Also interesting is the **Hôtel Hérouet,** the home of Jean Hérouet, treasurer of King Louis XIII, with its elegant octagonal turret built in 1510. At no. 31 is the **Hôtel d'Albret,** built in the 16th century but restored in the 17th, with a fine facade reconstructed in the 18th century. Further along, at the corner of Rue Pavée, is the **Hôtel Lamoignon.** Built in 1580 for Diane of France, the legitimised daughter of Henri II, in 1658 it became the residence of Lamoignon, president of Paris' first Parliament. Alphonse Daudet also lived there in the 19th century. The main body of the building is divided by six Corinthian pilasters, and the façade overlooks the courtyard. Here too is the **Historical Library of the City of Paris,** which has more than 500,000 documents.

HÔTEL CARNAVALET

Entrance to this mansion, one of the finest in the city and containing one of its most interesting museums, is at no. 23 Rue de Sévigné. Constructed in 1544, it was rebuilt in Renaissance forms in 1655 by François Mansart, who added a floor and gave it its present appearance; it also contains some fine statues by Jean Goujon. In 1677, the building was rented by the writer Marie de Rabutin, better known as the Marquise de Sévigné, and in the 19th century the Museum was opened, containing historical documents of great importance and rarity related to the history of Paris, seen through its historical figures, monuments and costumes, from Henri IV to our own time. Passing through the main entrance (16th century — the *lions* and the *cornucopia* on the keystone were carved by Jean Goujon), we reach the courtyard, in the centre of which is the *bronze statue of Louis XIV,* by Coysevox (1689). The building at the end is still in Gothic style, while the *reliefs of the Four Seasons* are Renaissance, the work of the school of Goujon.

CARNAVALET MUSEUM

Entrance to the museum is on the right of the courtyard. On the **first floor** are collections of furniture, works of art and paintings which illustrate the Paris of Louis XIV, Louis XV and Louis XVI. On the **ground floor,** on the other hand, most of the rooms are dedicated to the Revolution and the First Empire. Among the museum's most interesting relics are the bill of indictment of Louis XVI and the key of the Temple in which the royal family was imprisoned, the dressing table and chair used by Marie-Antoinette in the Tower of the Temple (on the table are perfume bottles and a miniature of the Dauphin which the queen made during her imprisonment), the shaving plate and razors of Louis, a game of tombola and an exercise book belonging to the Dauphin, a model of the guillotine, the page of the appeal which Robespierre was signing when he was arrested (the first two letters of his surname and his bloodstains can still be seen), the sword and epaulettes of La Fayette, and the Phrygian cap and pike belonging to Lefebvre.

PLACE DES VOSGES

Perfectly square, 354 feet long on each side, the square is completely surrounded by 36 old and picturesque mansions, with porticoes on the ground floor, surmounted by two orders of windows. In the centre of the square, among its trees and flower beds, is the *marble statue of Louis XIII on horseback,* a copy of the original by P. Biard destroyed during the Revolution. The square stands on the site of the Hôtel des Tournelles, where Henri II died in a joust in 1559. The square was designed by Henri IV in 1607 and completed in 1612. In the middle of the southern side is the splendid **Pavilion of the King,** built for Henri IV himself, and opposite it is the Pavilion of the Queen. At no. 1 bis Madame de Sévigné was born, at no. 21 Richelieu lived, at no. 6, the former **Hôtel de Rohan-Guémenée,** Victor Hugo lived from 1832 to 1848. Today this building contains the **Victor Hugo Museum,** in which are souvenirs and objects recalling the most important aspects of his life, besides 350 drawings which bear witness to his great and versatile genius.

RUE ST-ANTOINE – This is the continuation of Rue de Rivoli going as far as Place de la Bastille. Enlarged in the 14th century, it became a meeting place and fashionable promenade. Here in 1559 Henri II organised a joust to celebrate the marriage of his daughter, but he was wounded in the eye by the lance of the captain of his Scots Guards, Montgomery, and he died soon after being taken to the Hôtel des Tournelles.

ST-PAUL - ST-LOUIS

This is another fine example of the Jesuit-style church, the oldest in this style after that of the Carmelite monastery. It was built between 1627 and 1641, and took its Baroque inspiration from the church of Gesù in Rome. The façade, with its superimposed orders of columns, is so high that it hides the dome, a phenomenon rarely found elsewhere since in the later buildings (Dôme-des-Invalides, Sorbonne, Val-de-Grâce) the dome can clearly be seen.

Interior. The inside is well lit, without aisles but with linking chapels. Over the crossing is the fine cupola, on top of which is a lantern. The church contained many works of art, but these suffered great losses during the Revolution, when the reliquaries containing the hearts of Louis XIII and Louis XIV were melted down. In the transept are three panels of the 17th century, depicting *scenes from the life of St Louis.* The fourth, which has been lost, is substituted by one by Delacroix (1827), representing *Christ in the Garden of Olives.* A marble statue by Germain Pilon (16th century), depicting *Our Lady of Sorrows,* is in the chapel on the left of the chancel.

Also in Rue St-Antoine, at no. 62, is the **Hôtel de Béthune-Sully.** Built in 1624 by Du Cerceau, it was bought in 1634 by Béthune-Sully, former minister of Henri IV. Part of it today is the seat of the Historical Monuments Department. The *inner courtyard* is one of the finest examples of the Louis XIII style: the pediments are decorated and the dormer windows carved and enriched by a series of statues representing the *Elements* and the *Seasons.* A garden links the building with Place des Vosges.

The Column of July, in the centre of Place de la Bastille.

PLACE DE LA BASTILLE – Rue St-Antoine ends here, in this square famous for its memories of the Revolution. Here stood the massive fortress built under Charles V between 1370 and 1382. It later became a State prison in which, among others, the mysterious figure who became known as the Man in the Iron Mask was held. The ill-famed prison was thus the first and most important objective of the popular uprising which broke out on 14 July 1789, when 7000 enraged Parisians marched against what was considered the symbol of the monarchy's despotism. The Bastille, held by its governor De Launay with only 32 Swiss guards and 82 invalids, soon fell into the people's hands, and the governor was put to death and the prisoners (only seven) freed. The next day the demolition of the prison began, lasting until the following year. When the demolition was completed, the people danced on what had been the foundations of the terrible Bastille. Today there are lines on the paving stones of the square marking the outlines of the former fortress. In the centre of the square is the **July Column,** built between 1831 and 1840 in memory of the Parisians killed in July 1830. Their bodies, together with those who died in February 1848, are enclosed in the marble base, and their names are engraved on the shaft of the column. At the top of the column (which can be climbed via a stairway with 238 steps), 171 feet high, is the *figure of Liberty* and a platform commanding a splendid view of the Marais quarter, the Ile-de-la-Cité and the Ste Geneviève Hill.

120

The recent building which accomodates the Opéra de la Bastille.

Several boulevards radiate out from Place de la Bastille, including Boulevard Henri IV, at the end of which, almost on the Seine, is the **caserne des Célestins,** a former Benedictine monastery which today houses the barracks of the Republican Guards.

ARSENAL LIBRARY — Standing at no. 1 Rue de Sully, the building was constructed by Sully in 1594, while the reconstruction of the façade was done by Philibert Delorme. The library was created in 1757 by the War Minister, Marquis Paulmy d'Argenson, and later enriched by the Count d'Artois, the future Charles X. Today it contains more than $1^1/_2$ million volumes, 120,000 prints, 15,000 manuscripts, many illuminated manuscripts and important documents concerning the history of the theatre. Its rooms are decorated with fine paintings from the 18th century. An interesting visit is that to the apartment of Charles Nodier, who was librarian from 1824 to 1844.

HÔTEL DE SENS

Situated at no. 1 Rue du Figuier, this is the only other example in Paris, after the Hôtel de Cluny, of the great medieval private mansions. It was built between 1475 and 1507 as the residence of the archbishops of Sens (of which Paris was a dependence until 1622). It was considerably restored in 1911, when it became the property of the city of Paris.

The façade is embellished at the corners by cylindrical turrets, and has Guelph windows and dormer windows with Flamboyant Gothic decoration. Through the entrance with its pointed arch, one enters the courtyard, with its square tower containing a staircase. In the Hôtel de Sens is the **Forney Library,** containing documents of a technical and scientific nature and collections of posters.

ITINERARY 9

FROM PLACE DU CHÂTELET *(Châtelet station)* **TO PLACE DE LA RÉPUBLIQUE.**

Place du Châtelet – **St-Jacques Tower** – St-Merri – **Fountain of the Innocents** – Bourse de Commerce – **Forum des Halles** – **Beaubourg** – National Museum of Modern Art – National Museum of Technics – **St-Eustache** – Rue de Turbigo – Tower of Jean-sans-Peur – Rue St-Denis – St-Leu-St-Gilles – St-Nicolas-des-Champs – Conservatoire des Arts et Métiers – Place Igor Stravinsky – Square du Temple – Place de la République.

PLACE DU CHÂTELET

The square takes its name from the ancient fortress, the Grand Châtelet, built to defend the Pont au Change in front of it and destroyed under Napoleon I. But the present appearance of the square dates from the time of Napoleon III. In the centre is the **Châtelet Fountain** (also called the Fountain of Victory or of the Palm), with its base adorned by sphinxes and statues, dating from 1858. The column was erected in 1808 to celebrate the victories of Napoleon I. On either side of the square are two theatres, both designed by Davioud. On the right (standing with one's back to the Seine) is the **Théâtre de la Ville** and on the left the **Théâtre du Châtelet,** which with seating for 3600 has the largest auditorium in Paris.

Place du Châtelet.

St-Jacques Tower.

ST-JACQUES TOWER

Dominating the whole square, the tower is all that is left of the old church of St-Jacques-la-Boucherie, destroyed in 1797. Erected between 1508 and 1522, it is 171 feet high and its style belongs to the purest Flamboyant Gothic. It has narrow windows alternating with niches surmounted by spires and pinnacles, within which are many statues. The statue on the top of the tower represents *St James the Greater* (Chenillon, 1870). Another statue, depicting *Pascal,* stands at the base of the tower, under the vaults, in memory of the experiments on the weight of air which he made in 1648. The tower today contains two weather stations.

ST-MERRI — Entrance to the church of St-Merri, or St Medericus, who died here in the 7th century, is at no. 76 Rue de la Verrerie. The church, begun in 1520 and completed in 1612, is strangely enough in the earlier Flamboyant Gothic style. The façade underwent various works of remodelling in the 17th and 18th centuries, and today has a portal adorned with modern statues; alongside the church is the 17th-century bell tower.

Interior. With four aisles, the interior too, like the façade, was remodelled at various stages: under Louis XV, the architect Boffrand and the Slodtz brothers demolished the roodscreen, transformed the pointed arches into round arches and covered the pillars of the chancel with gilded stuccoes and marble. The fine 16th-century stained glass in the transept and chancel and the ribbed vault over the transept crossing remain. The church also contains some fine works of art: a 17th-century organ, a *Virgin and Child* by Van Loo and the wood inlays by the Slodtz brothers in the chancel and sacristy.

THE FOUNTAIN OF THE INNOCENTS – This is one of the masterpieces of French Renaissance. Designed by Pierre Lescot and sculpted by Jean Goujon, it is the oldest fountain in Paris. It was erected between 1547 and 1550 as a square structure, with Classical arcades on each side and many bas reliefs of nymphs, marine gods, tritons and Victories. The fountain originally stood at the corner of Rue St Denis and the present Rue Berger, where it was against a wall so that only three sides were visible. The fourth side was sculpted by Pajou and added in 1788, when the fountain was moved to where it still stands today.

BOURSE DU COMMERCE – The Hôtel de Nesle during the 12th century and the Hôtel de la Reyne under Catherine de' Medici, the Bourse du Commerce is an important construction of a circular shape with a central courtyard covered by a glass and steel dome overlooking a huge room, 1.200 metres square: from here one can see the Stock Exchange offices, laid out in a crown-like way on two floors of balconies.

Behind the Stock Exchange building stretch the gardens which belonged to the Hôtel de la Reyne: in the plans for the complete restructurization of the district, this beautiful green zone will cover an area of five hectares and will ideally join the Stock Exchange to the Pompidou Centre. Underneath these gardens there are three levels which, according to the plans, will hold an auditorium, a video centre, the House of Music and Dance for the city of Paris and a car park which will be able to hold up to eight hundred cars.

FORUM DES HALLES

Les Halles, the oldest district of Paris, is also the liveliest and most vivacious. Emilie Zola once described it, with a colourful expression, as the "belly of Paris": in fact, the city wholesale grocery market once stood here: ten pavilions of iron, steel and cast iron. When the market was transferred to Rungis in March 1969, the district seemed suddenly to have lost all of its vivacity as well as its main purpose. It needed new life: and so began the biggest transformation work ever carried out in the heart of a city. A huge hole was made at the feet of the Gothic Church

View of the Forum.

View of Georges Pompidou Centre.

of St Eustache from which, for around 8 months, a good thirty lorries a day carried away a million cubic metres of earth. Within this new concept of urban space, in the place where the city used to go to feed itself, there now rose a new form of culture and commerce: the Forum, over forty thousand square metres of glass and aluminium, marble stairways and furniture, developed over four underground levels and around a quadrangular open-air square. Inaugurated on 4th September 1979 and based on a project by two architects, Claude Vasconi and Georges Pencreac'h, it can truly be said that the Forum has everything: on the first level there are shops for clothes, objets d'art and gastronomy; the second level contains everything for the house; the third level has places of entertainment, restaurants and ten cinemas; the fourth level has banks and information centres. Almost the entire commercial centre area faces onto covered galleries of large windows, so that the daylight penetrates to all the levels. There is also an underground station linked to four lines of the métro and two lines of the RER.

THE GEORGES POMPIDOU CENTRE (BEAUBOURG)

For nearly all visitors and tourists, the "Georges Pompidou National Centre of Art and Culture" is today, simply, the Beaubourg.
Situated between Rue Rambuteau and Rue Saint-Merri and between Rue St Martin and Rue Renard, the Beaubourg, with

its audacious architecture, is now a part of our culture and civilization. In 1969, the then President of the Republic, Georges Pompidou, decided to create an important cultural centre in the area known as the "plateau Beaubourg". An international call to tender was announced and 49 countries participated with 681 projects: the project of Renzo Piano and Richard Rogers was accepted. Building began in April 1972 and the centre was opened by Giscard d'Estaing on the 31st January 1977. The building, an "urban machine", as it has often been described, occupies an area of one hundred metres square. With a revolutionary idea, all the structures normally situated inside a building such as escalators, lifts, safety exits and vertical canalizations, here have been situated on the outside. This idea of the general evolution of spaces is continued on the inside: every expression of contemporary art is a part of our lives and should be accessible to everyone at any time. The Beaubourg is not intended to be a museum with works of art but instead a place for meeting and exchanging ideas between artists and the public, the public and the things, where everyone can freely move around and approach the principal expressions of contemporary art and culture. Some curious pieces of information: the Beaubourg is higher and longer than the Parthenon of the Athens Acropolis (it is in fact 42 metres high and 166 metres long); it weighs 15.000 tons of steel compared with the 7.000 tons of iron in the Eiffel Tower; each external pipeline is painted a different colour because each colour corresponds to a different function: blue corresponds to the climatization plant, yellow the electrical installation, red the circulation and green the water circuits. The various departments in the Beaubourg are also indicated by different colours: yellow indicates the common spaces, the forum and general services; green is for the public information Library (with over one million items made up of books, documents, slides, records and microfilms spread out over three floors: no entrance card is needed here, everyone is free to choose the book they want); blue corresponds to the Industrial Inventions Centre; violet is for the famous IRCAM, the Institute for Acustic-Musical Coordination and Research, eight thousand metres square of rooms, laboratories and studios dedicated to the creation of modern music; and finally, red corresponds to the National Museum of Modern Art.

THE NATIONAL MUSEUM OF MODERN ART – This Museum occupies the top three floors of the Pompidou Centre and contains works from the National Centre of Contemporary Arts as well as those previously exhibited in the Avenue Président Wilson Museum. The new internal architecture of the collections was designed by the Italian architect, Gae Aulenti. This Museum features the most significant works of the 20th century: at the entrance there is H. Rousseau's *Snake Charmer* and works by Kandinsky and Picasso; there follow rooms dedicated to the groups of "Fauves" (works by Derain, Vlaminck, Dufy and Matisse) and Germain painters of the "Die Brücke" group, including Kirchner and Emil Nolde. Cubism is documented in particular by Picasso (*the Guitarist, Nature Morte à la tête Antique, Minotaur*, from 1927, the famous *Harlequin*, 1923), Braque *(Woman with Mandolin)*, Giorgio Morandi (various *Still Lifes*) and Juan Gris. There is an important Italian (Carrà, Magnelli, Severini and De

View of St. Eustaches' Church.

Chirico) and Russian representation (pictures and sculptures by Archipenko). There are many works by Kandinsky and Matisse: of Kandinsky's works we mention the *Park of Saint-Cloud, Old City, Improvisation no. 14, Blue Sky, Mutual Agreement, Accent in Pink;* there are numerous bronzes by Matisse: *Interior with Goldfish Bowl, Violinist at the Window, Grande Intérieur Rouge, Still Life with Magnolia, Interior at Nice.* There are many works by Fernand Léger, including the monumental *Composition with Two Parrots,* which he began in 1933 and finished in 1939. Then there is Piet Mondrian and his *Compositions;* Paul Klee with *Florentine Villas* and *Mask of a Young Idol;* Marc Chagall with the *Soul of the City* and *The War; Clowns* by Georges Rouault. Surrealism is represented by Max Ernst, René Magritte, Y. Tanguy, Salvador Dalí, Picabia, Mirò and André Breton. Finally there is contemporary art with works by Dubuffet, Jackson Pollock, Mark Rothko, Lucio Fontana, the exponents of American Pop Art (Claes Oldenburg, Roy Lichtenstein, Andy Warhol), Op Art (with kinetic works by Vasarely and Soto), the Cobra movement, works by Francis Bacon, right up to the latest exponents of New Realism and Hyperrealism.

PLACE IGOR STRAVINSKY – Situated between Place Georges Pompidou and Rue du Cloitre Sainte-Merri, the Place Igor Stravinsky has recently been inaugurated. It is almost completely taken up by an original, colourful and amusing fountain by Tinguely, the kinetic sculptor belonging to the Nouveau Réalisme group, officially formed in Paris on the 27th October 1960.

ST-EUSTACHE

Considered the most beautiful church in Paris after Notre-Dame, St-Eustache stands at the edge of Les Halles. Its construction continued over a long period of time. In 1532 the foundation stone was laid, but only in 1637 could the church be said to be complete. Designed by Lemercier, it combines in an original way a Gothic structure with Renaissance decoration. The passage from one style to the other can be followed best of all in the sides and in the apse, which have three orders of windows, tall pilasters and great flying arches, while the rose windows are typical of the Renaissance.

Interior. Its dimensions are imposing: 328 feet long, 144 feet wide and 108 feet high. It has double aisles around the nave, with transept and chancel. The round Renaissance arcades in the nave are divided by bundle pillars, while the vaulting of the nave, chancel and transept is in the Flamboyant Gothic style. A great organ, made in 1844, stands above the entrance, and important concerts are still given in the church. In a chapel in the chancel is the *tomb of Colbert*, the famous Minister of Finance under Louis XIV: the sepulchre was designed by Le Brun, Coysevox sculpted the statues of Colbert and Abundance and Tuby that of Fidelity. Works by Rubens, Luca Giordano and the Sienese Manetti can be found in other chapels.

RUE DE TURBIGO — This street leads from the Les Halles quarter to Place de la République. Nearby, after Rue Etienne Marcel, is the **Tower of Jean-sans-Peur,** today incorporated in a school building (at no. 20 Rue de Turbigo). Square in form and crowned with overhanging battlements (from which boiling oil used to be poured), it was erected in 1408 by Jean-sans-Peur (John the Fearless) following the assassination of the Duke of Orléans, ordered by him.

RUE ST-DENIS — Built in the 7th century, Rue St-Denis soon became the most wealthy street in Paris. Along it the kings moved in solemn procession when they entered Paris to go to Notre-Dame; this was also the street along which the dead were taken to be buried at St-Denis.

ST-LEU-ST-GILLES — The church, at no. 92 Rue St-Denis, is dedicated to two saints of the 6th century, St Lupus, the bishop of Sens, and St Giles, a hermit from Provence. Its construction goes back to 1320, but it has been much restored and remodelled. Two towers with cusps stand at the sides of the façade; the bell tower on the left was added in 1858.

Interior. The vaults in the nave are in the Gothic style, while the chancel is Classical and higher than the nave. It has some fine works of art, including the keystones of the vaults, a 16th-century marble group representing the *Virgin and St Anne,* and some alabaster bas reliefs at the entrance to the sacristy, brought here from the former Cemetery of the Innocents.

ST-NICOLAS-DES-CHAMPS — Standing in Rue St-Martin, another of the streets which cross Rue Turbigo, this is dedicated to St Nicholas, a 4th-century bishop from Asia Minor. It was built in the 12th century, reconstructed in the 15th century and further enlarged in following centuries. The façade and bell tower, fine examples of the Flamboyant Gothic style, have been restored. On the right-hand side, there is a splendid Renaissance **portal** (1581), the graceful forms of which may be a copy of one of the doors of the Hôtel des Tournelles. The apse too, with its large windows, is an imposing Renaissance structure.

After leaving the church, in Rue Volta no. 3, we find the **oldest house** in Paris, dating back as far as the 13th or 14th century.

CONSERVATOIRE DES ARTS ET MÉTIERS — At no. 292 Rue St-Martin, this was once the site of the Abbey of St-Martin-des-Champs, built in 1061 and reconstructed in the 13th century. The Conservatory of Arts and Professions, created in 1794, took over this site in 1799; today it includes a school and museum. Of the former abbey, only the refectory and chancel remain today. Through the entrance one reaches the main courtyard, on the right of which is the **refectory** of the old monastery, now used as a library. This 13th-century refectory is a masterpiece by Pierre de Montreuil. Measuring 141 feet by 39 feet and gracefully divided down the centre by seven slender columns, the hall has the purest of Gothic lines. Its tall mullioned windows, Gothic vaulting and perfect proportions make it a splendid work. Halfway along the right side is a door, on the outside of which are fine carvings. The **National Museum of**

Technics is reached from the courtyard via a stairway; it contains machinery and models which document the progress made by science and industry.

GROUND FLOOR – In **Room 2** are the most important equipment and personal effects of the great chemist Lavoisier. **From Room 4 to Room 9:** objects to do with metallurgy and steel making, displaying various techniques, from the mining of ore to the use of blast furnaces. **Room 10** consists of the 13th-century nave of the church of St-Martin-des-Champs (the façade of which can be seen beyond the refectory, while the apse is on the other side of Rue Réaumur): the chancel, built between 1130 and 1140, clearly shows in the cruciform and ogival vaults the transition from Romanesque to Gothic. In this room various means of locomotion are exhibited, from the first bicycles to the first automobiles, from the first scooter to the flying machine in which Blériot crossed the English Channel. Suspended from the ceiling is the pendulum with which Léon Foucault demonstrated that the earth rotates. **Room 11** has exhibits illustrating the introduction of machinery to agriculture; **Room 13** instruments of geodesy and topography; **Room 15** the earliest automata, including the famous *Joueuse de Tympanon*, made in 1784, which belonged to Marie-Antoinette – a small puppet, representing a woman playing Gluck airs on the dulcimer, the favourite plaything queen's. **From Room 16** to **20** there are instruments of astronomy and watchmaking; in **Room 21,** railways exhibits.

FIRST FLOOR – **Room 23:** two examples of Pascal's arithmetic machine; **Room 24:** turbines, boilers, etc.; **Rooms 26** and **27:** models related to electricity and physics; **Rooms 28** and **29:** glass; **from Room 30** to **34:** objects related to optics, acoustics and mechanics; **Rooms 35** to **40:** dedicated to radar, television, communications via satellite, electronic acoustics, photography and the laser (among the exhibits is the first film projector made by the Lumière brothers); **Room 46:** graphic arts (printing presses, typewriters) and technology of everyday life (from elevators to various types of heating); **from Room 47** to **49:** spinning and weaving.

SQUARE DU TEMPLE – On this site there once stood a vast complex of buildings, occupied by the religious and military order of the Knights Templar. Founded in 1118 in the Holy Land, the order was established in Paris in 1140 and grew swiftly. The Knights Templar were independent of the crown and came to own the entire Marais quarter, forming a powerful financial group which soon constituted a real state within the state. On 13 October 1307, Philippe the Fair had all the Knights Templar in France imprisoned, and in 1314 had their Grand Master, Jacques de Molay, and his followers burnt at the stake. The order was thus suppressed, and the Templar buildings passed into the hands of the Hospitaliers de St-Jean-de-Jérusalem, or Knights of St John of Jerusalem, the original name of the Knights of Malta. This order too was suppressed by the Revolution, and the Temple became the prison of the royal family. On 13 August 1792, Louis XVI, Marie-Antoinette, their two children and the king's sister were closed in the Temple Tower, nearly 150 feet high with walls 10 feet thick. After the execution of the royal family, in order to avoid the site attracting Royalist pilgrimages, it was decided in 1808 to demolish the Tower. The whole area was gradually transformed into an open-air market, particularly of old clothes, known as the **Carreau du Temple.** In 1857, the square was remodelled by Haussmann as it stands today, including the covered market.

PLACE DE LA RÉPUBLIQUE – Laid out by Haussmann in 1854, the square today is a vast bottleneck of traffic. In the centre is the **monument to the Republic,** erected by Morice in 1883. On the base are large bronze bas reliefs by Dalou, representing the great events in the history of the Republic.

Porte St-Martin.

Porte St-Denis.

FROM PLACE DE LA RÉPUBLIQUE *(République station)* TO PLACE DU TERTRE.

Boulevard St-Martin – **Porte St-Martin** – **Porte St-Denis** – **Notre-Dame-de-Bonne-Nouvelle** – Boulevard Montmartre – Grevin Museum – Boulevard des Italiens – Opéra-Comique – Rue Lafayette – Boulevard Haussmann – **Chapelle Expiatoire** – Place St-Augustin – Church of St-Augustin – Jacquemart-André Museum – Cathedral of St-Alexandre-Newski – Parc Monceau – Cernuschi Museum – Nissim de Camondo Museum – Museum of the Conservatoire de Musique – Place de Clichy – **Montmartre** – Cemetery – Place Blanche – Moulin Rouge – Place Pigalle – St-Jean-de-Montmartre – Rue Lepic – Moulin de la Galette – **Sacré-Cœur** – St-Pierre-de-Montmartre – **Place du Tertre** – « Au lapin agile ».

THE GREAT BOULEVARDS

These famous avenues extend for some two miles in a wide sweep from Place de la Bastille to the Madeleine. As they now are, they were laid out last century by Haussmann. The boulevards had originally replaced the old Charles V city walls, stretching from the Bastille to the Gate of St-Denis, and the ramparts of Charles IX and Louis XIII, which went from the St-Denis Gate to the Madeleine, demolished in the late 17th century. The boulevards were much frequented throughout the 19th and until the early years of the 20th century, when fashionable crowds filled the luxurious cafés, shops and theatres which lined these wide streets. Today their fashionable character has been transformed into a more noisy and popular atmosphere.

BOULEVARD ST-MARTIN – This boulevard goes from Place de la République to Porte St-Martin. It contains many cinemas and theatres, including the **Théâtre de la Renaissance** (1872) and alongside the **Théâtre de la Porte St-Martin,** built in 1781. The latter has remained famous because of the triumphant performances there by the great Sarah Bernhardt and Coquelin in the role of Cyrano (1897).

PORTE ST-MARTIN

A triumphal arch 56 feet high, it was erected by Bullet in 1674 to commemorate the taking of Besançon and the defeat of the Spanish, Dutch and German armies. It has three vaults, and is covered with bas reliefs carved by Le Hongre, Desjardins, Legros and Marsy and representing on one side the *capture of Besançon* and the *breaking of the Triple Alliance* and on the other the *capture of Limbourg* and the *defeat of the Germans.*

PORTE ST-DENIS

This gate too, like the Porte St-Martin, has the form of a triumphal arch, with a single vault, measuring 79 feet both in height and in width. Designed by Blondel and erected in 1672, it has sculpture by the Anguier brothers and was intended to celebrate the victories of Louis XIV in Germany, when in less than two months the French king succeeded in conquering forty strongholds. The allegorical bas reliefs representing Holland and the Rhine are fine works.

After the Porte St-Denis, the boulevard takes the name of **Boulevard de Bonne-Nouvelle.** A stairway on the right leads up to the **church of Notre-Dame-de-Bonne-Nouvelle,** its bell tower being all that remains of the church rebuilt under Anne of Austria. Inside, apart from a fine *statue of the Virgin* (17th century), are two original 18th-century panels, attributed to Mignard: *Henrietta of England with her three children before St Francis of Sales* and *Anne of Austria and Henrietta of England.*

After **Boulevard Poissonnière,** we reach **Boulevard Montmartre,** one of Paris' busiest streets, running from Rue Montmartre to Boulevard des Italiens. At no. 10 is the **Grévin Museum,** founded in 1882 by the caricaturist Grévin, containing all sorts of magic devices and amusements, including waxworks of great figures and famous scenes in history. Near the museum, at no. 7, is the **Théâtre des Variétés,** home of vaudeville and light opera, in which many of the works by composers such as Offenbach, Tristan Bernard and Sacha Guitry were performed.

BOULEVARD DES ITALIENS — This boulevard's period of maximum splendour began during the time of the Directory and continued until the end of the Second Empire. Great financiers, famous journalists and distinguished men of letters frequented its cafés, the Café Anglais, the Café Tortoni and the Café Riche (the latter unfortunately has disappeared: in its place, at no. 16, is the Banque Nationale de Paris).

OPÉRA-COMIQUE — Standing at the end of the boulevard in Place Boieldieu, it was rebuilt after two fires by Bernier in 1898. The comic operas from the Italian repertory were performed here in the past, works by such composers as Mascagni, Rossini and Leoncavallo.

RUE LAFAYETTE — This street begins from Boulevard Haussmann, and on the corner are the Galeries Lafayette, one of the largest department stores in the city. The crossroads where it meets Rue Le Peletier was the scene of the attempt on Napoleon III by Felice Orsini on 14 January 1858.

BOULEVARD HAUSSMANN — The boulevard is named after the man who was largely responsible for replanning the city of Paris, Baron G. E. Haussmann, prefect of the Seine from 1853 to 1870. The wide avenue, begun in 1857, was completed in 1926. At no. 26 is the house where Marcel Proust lived from 1906 to 1919.

CHAPELLE EXPIATOIRE

The Expiatory Chapel is in the Square Louis XVI, surrounded by a green and tranquil garden. Here there was a small cemetery, dating from 1722, in which were buried the Swiss Guards who fell on 10 August 1792 at the Tuileries and the victims of the guillotine, a total of 1343 persons, including Louis XVI and Marie-Antoinette, whose bodies were later transferred, on 21 January 1815, to St-Denis. Louis XVIII also had Fontaine build this chapel between 1815 and 1826. In front of it is a cloister and a small garden, and on the right the tombs of Charlotte Corday and Philippe-Egalité. Inside the chapel are two marble groups: one by Bosio (1826) representing *Louis XVI,* and another by Cortot (1836) of *Marie-Antoinette sustained by Religion,* which has the features of the king's sister Elisabeth.

Boulevard des Italiens.

Boulevard des Capucines.

PLACE ST-AUGUSTIN – The square is at the point where Boulevard Haussmann and Boulevard Malesherbes meet. It is dominated by the imposing mass of the **church of St-Augustin,** built by Baltard between 1860 and 1871 in a curious mixture of Byzantine and Renaissance styles. In it metal girders were used for the first time in a church.

JACQUEMART-ANDRÉ MUSEUM – The museum is in an elegant late 19th-century building at no. 158 Boulevard Haussmann, which the owner, Mme Nélie Jacquemart-André, left to the Institut de France in 1912. It contains large collections of 18th-century European and Italian Renaissance works. On the ground floor are paintings and drawings by Boucher, Chardin and Watteau and sculpture by Houdon and Pigalle, recalling the era of Louis XV, while the 17th and 18th centuries are well represented by Canaletto, Murillo, Rembrandt and others. The Italian works include Botticelli, terracotta pieces by the Della Robbia family, sculpture by Con '' and large canvases by Tintoretto and Paolo Uccello.

CATHEDRAL OF ST-ALEXANDRE-NEWSKY – This is the Russian Orthodox church of Paris. At no. 12 Rue Daru, it was built in 1860 in the Neo-Byzantine style of Moscow's churches. The interior is embellished with gilded stuccoes, icons and frescoes.

PARC MONCEAU – This splendid garden, its main entrance on Boulevard de Courcelles, is the centre of a fashionable part of the city. The park was laid out by the painter Carmontelle for the Duke of Orléans in 1778. On 22 October 1797, the first parachutist in the world, Garnerin, landed in the park. In 1852 the financier Pereire had two splendid mansions built here, and later the engineer Alphand opened up part of it as an English-style public garden, with ruins, small temples, a tiny lake and imitation rocks. At the entrance is the Pavilion of Chartres, a rotunda with columns designed by Ledoux. The oval **Naumachia** basin has a colonnade around it, brought from the mausoleum of Henri II at St-Denis, which was never completed. Nearby is a Renaissance-style arcade, originally part of the Hôtel de Ville.

CERNUSCHI MUSEUM – Its entrance at no. 7 Avenue Velasquez, this was the residence of the banker Cernuschi, who in 1896 left it in his will to the city of Paris, along with the works of Oriental art which he had collected. These include important Neolithic terracottas, bronzes and jade. Worth seeing are a fine stone statue representing a *Seated Bodhisattva*, from the 5th century, and several precious works of ancient painting, including the *Horse and Grooms,* a masterpiece of 18th-century Tang painting on silk.

NISSIM DE CAMONDO MUSEUM – This museum, at no. 63 Rue de Monceau, was the residence of the Count de Camondo, who left it and his collections of 18th-century art to the nation in 1936 in memory of his son Nissim, who had died in the war. The mansion is a magnificent and accurate example of a typically elegant dwelling in the era of Louis XVI. It contains pieces of furniture by the greatest cabinetmakers, clocks and silverware, splendid dinner services and canvases by Guardi, Jongkind, Vibée-Lebrun and others.

MUSEUM OF THE CONSERVATOIRE DE MUSIQUE – At no. 14 Rue de Madrid, the museum is part of the Conservatory of Music. It contains about 2000 pieces, including a great many fine and historic instruments: Stradivarius violins, the harp which belonged to Marie-Antoinette, the piano on which Rouget de Lisle played his composition, the Marseillaise, and Beethoven's clavichord. On the floor above is a music library which contains rare scores, including that of Mozart's "Don Giovanni".

PLACE DE CLICHY – This busy square, always filled with people and traffic, was the scene of furious fighting in March 1814 between the Russian troops, who had entered Paris with the other Allies and had their bivouac in the Champs-Élysées, and Marshal Moncey, to whom the monument was later erected in the centre of the square. It also stands at the beginning of Boulevard de Clichy and Boulevard de Rochechouart, which runs around the base of the hill of Montmartre.

Panoramic view of the hill of Montmartre from Notre-Dame.

MONTMARTRE

Montmartre was and is one of the most picturesque and curious quarters of Paris. It stands on a limestone hill 425 feet high where, according to the legend, St Denis, the first bishop of Paris, was beheaded in about 250 A.D., along with the priests Eleutherius and Rusticus.

Because of its strategic position, dominating the whole of Paris, Montmartre has also had an important part in the city's political history. In fact the Commune began from an incident here in March 1871. Then throughout the 19th century Montmartre was the mecca of all the Bohemian artists and for a long time it maintained its place as the literary and artistic centre of the whole city.

MONTMARTRE CEMETERY — The entrance is in Avenue Rachel. Opened in 1795, it contains the tombs of many famous figures: painters like Fragonard, Degas and Chassériau; writers such as Théophile Gautier, Edmond and Jules de Goncourt, Stendhal, Emile Zola, Alexandre Dumas the Younger and Heinrich Heine, and the composers Hector Berlioz and Offenbach. There are also the tombs of the playwrights Labiche and Giraudoux, the actors Sacha Guitry and Louis Jouvet, the celebrated Russian ballet dancer Nijinsky, and the famous Alphonsine Plessis, better known as the "Lady of the Camelias".

The Moulin Rouge.

PLACE BLANCHE — Lying at the foot of the Montmartre hill, it owes its name, meaning "White Square", to the chalk roads which once existed here. It is overlooked by the long sails of the **Moulin Rouge,** the music hall founded in 1889; among the artists who performed on its stage were Jane Avril, Valentin le Désossé and La Goulue, and here the can-can was born, immortalised in the canvases of Toulouse-Lautrec.

From here, by way of Boulevard de Clichy, lined by many modern cinemas and beer halls, one reaches **Place Pigalle,** a bustling scene, particularly at night, when its night clubs turn on their many lights. **Boulevard de Roche-chouart,** which begins here, is also filled with places of entertainment, including the dance hall, the Boule-Noire, at no. 120, and Taverne Bavaroise in front of it. At no. 84 was the famous **Chat-Noir** cabaret, recalled so often in the songs of Aristide Bruant, founded in 1881.

ST-JEAN-DE-MONTMARTRE — Near Square Jehan-Rictus, it was completed in 1904 by de Baudot, and is interesting as the first church in Paris built with reinforced concrete. It is known to the people of the area as St-Jean-des-Briques (St John of the Bricks) because of its brick exterior.

THE BATEAU-LAVOIR — Continuing by way of Rue Ravignan, we reach a small square, Place Emile-Goudeau. This was the site of the Bateau-Lavoir, a small wooden building unfortunately destroyed by a fire in 1970, where modern painting and poetry were born in about 1900. In it Picasso, Braque and Gris worked (Picasso painted the *Demoiselles d'Avignon,* which marked the birth of Cubism, here), and while they were revolutionising the traditional canons of painting, Max Jacob and Apollinaire were doing the same for poetry.

RUE LEPIC — It begins in Place Blanche and winds up towards the top of the hill. In autumn there is a veteran car rally which follows the street's steep curves. At no. 54 Vincent Van Gogh lived with his brother Theo. Nearby is the celebrated **Moulin de la Galette,** the last remaining windmill dating back to the 17th century and a former dance hall, which inspired paintings by Renoir and Van Gogh.

View of Pigalle by night.

SACRÉ-CŒUR

Standing majestically on the top of the Montmartre hill, it was begun in 1876 by national subscription and consecrated in 1919. The architects who designed it (among them Abadie and Magne) built it in a curious style, a mixture of Romanesque and Byzantine. The four small domes and the large central dome, standing on the high drum, are typically Oriental. On the back part, the square bell tower 275 feet high contains the **Savoyarde,** a bell weighing 19 tons, one of the largest in the world. An imposing stairway leads up to the façade of the church, in front of which is a porch with three arches; above are the *equestrian statues of King Louis the Blessed* and *Joan of Arc.*

Interior. Its dimensions are impressive and the decorations of sculpture, paintings and mosaics are extremely elaborate. From inside the church, the visitor can descend to visit the the crypt and can also climb up to the top of the dome, from which there is a magnificent panoramic view of Paris and the surrounding areas.

Artists at Place du Tertre.

To admire the white mass of Sacré-Cœur from a better vantage point, one should descend, either via the cable railway or down the ramps of steps, into Place St-Pierre below.

ST-PIERRE-DE-MONTMARTRE – This church is what is left of the abbey established by the Benedictine nuns at Montmartre. It was begun towards 1134 and completed by the end of the century. The façade was almost completely remodelled in the 18th century.

Interior. On the inside of the entrance wall are four columns which came from a Roman temple which previously occupied the site. The church has three aisles divided by pillars, a transept and three apses. In the left aisle is the *tomb of Adélaïde of Savoy,* wife of Louis VI the Big, who founded the abbey.

PLACE DU TERTRE

This old square, once used as a meeting place and now lined with trees, is the heart of Montmartre, animated by warmth and colour. It is frequented by painters and a cosmopolitan crowd and comes alive particularly at night, when its cafés and night clubs fill with people and the small space in the centre of the square fills with artists, who work a little for themselves and a great deal for the tourists.

"AU LAPIN AGILE" – Walking down Rue Norvins, we come to the steep and picturesque Rue des Saules. In this area lived some of the most famous Parisian painters, among them Suzanne Valadon and Utrillo. On the corner of Rue St-Vincent, half hidden by an acacia tree, is the rustic cabaret, "Au lapin agile", which was originally called the "Cabaret des Assassins" but which derived its present name ("At the Sign of the Agile Rabbit") from the sign painted by the artist Gill. Much frequented from 1908 to 1914 by penniless painters and poets who were soon to become celebrities, it is still today the scene of interesting literary gatherings.

Place du Tertre: the church of St-Pierre and the domes of Sacré-Coeur.

FROM THE PÈRE-LACHAISE CEMETERY *(Métro: lines 2 and 3 – Père-Lachaise station)* **TO VINCENNES.**

Père-Lachaise Cemetery – Place de la Nation – **Vincennes.**

PÈRE-LACHAISE CEMETERY

This is the largest and most important cemetery in Paris, because of the many tombs of illustrious men within its tranquil walls. On a hill, its grounds cover some 115 acres and were originally property acquired in 1626 by the Jesuits, who built there a rest home for their order. The present name derives from the confessor of Louis XIV, Father La Chaise, who often stayed there. In 1763 the Jesuits were dispossessed and the property was acquired by the city and in 1803,

PÈRE-LACHAISE CEMETERY: **the tomb of Frederick Chopin.**

Place de la Nation, with the bronze group depicting the Triumph of the Republic.

under Napoleon, it was transformed into a cemetery. It was the scene of the final, ferocious episode of the Commune, on 28 May 1871, when the last 147 defenders of the Commune, cornered in the cemetery the day before, were shot against the cemetery wall (now called the *Federalists' Wall*). A visit to the tombs becomes almost a historical pilgrimage through the realms of painting, poetry and philosophy. Among them are the tombs of the writers *De Musset, Molière, La Fontaine, Alphonse Daudet, the Hugo family, Beaumarchais, Paul Eluard, Oscar Wilde, Marcel Proust, Guillaume Apollinaire* and *Balzac;* the composers *Chopin* (his heart is in Warsaw), *Bizet, Dukas* and *Cherubini;* the painters *Géricault, David, Corot, Modigliani, Delacroix, De Nittis, Ingres, Daumier* and *Seurat;* the philosophers and scientists *F. Arago, Auguste Comte, Gay-Lussac, Allan Kardec* (founder of the philosophy of the spirit), *Abelard and Heloïse;* the political and military leaders *Masséna, Ney, Blanqui, Lecomte, Murat and Caroline Bonaparte;* the actresses and singers *Edith Piaf, Sarah Bernhardt* and *Adelina Patti,* and the dancer *Isadora Duncan.*

PLACE DE LA NATION — Formerly called Place du Trône, because of the great throne erected here on 26 August 1660 for Louis XIV and his young wife, Maria-Theresa, on their entrance into Paris. During the Revolution, the throne was torn down and the guillotine erected in its place: the square was thus renamed Place du Trône-Renversé (Square of the Overturned Throne). It was given its present name in 1880, when France's national day, the 14th of July, was first celebrated here. In the centre of the square today, surrounded by flower beds, is a basin with the *bronze group representing the Triumph of the Republic*, sculpted by Dalous for Place de la République but erected here in 1899. At the sides of Avenue du Trône, which begins here, are the two columns erected by Ledoux and surmounted by the *statues of Philippe Auguste and St Louis*. This avenue, which becomes Cours de Vincennes, leads directly to Vincennes, the large residential suburb, with its splendid park and magnificent castle.

VINCENNES

CASTLE — This was called the "Versailles of the Middle Ages" and its history is closely linked to the history of France. The Forest of Vincennes was acquired by the crown in the 11th century and Philippe Auguste had a manorhouse built there, to which Louis IX added the Chapel. The castle, built by the Valois, was begun by Philippe VI in 1334 and completed by Charles V in 1370: in this period the **keep,** part of the Chapel and the surrounding walls were constructed. In 1654 Mazarin (who had become governor of Vincennes two years before) commissioned Le Vau to erect two symmetrical pavilions for the King and Queen. From the beginning of the 16th century up until 1784, the monarchs preferred Versailles to Vincennes, and the keep, where they had previously resided, became a state prison. In 1738 it became a porcelain factory (transferred to Sèvres in 1756), and Napoleon I converted it into a powerful arsenal, where in 1814, under its governor, General Daumensil, it opposed a heroic resistance to the Allies. It was modified by Louis-Philippe, who made it a rampart in the city's defences, and then its restoration was begun by Viollet-le-Duc under Napoleon III. Unfortunately the castle was seriously damaged on 24 August 1944, when the Germans blew up part of its fortifications and set fire to the King and Queen's pavilions.

The castle is built in the form of a great rectangle, surrounded by a deep moat and formidable walls, on which there are towers which have been reduced in height. The entrance tower, the **Tour du Village,** is the only one apart from the keep which has not been lopped: it is 138 feet high and although the statues which adorned the outside of it have been lost remains of Gothic decoration above the entrance portal can still be seen.

On the west side stands the magnificent **keep,** the sturdy but graceful lines of which convey the essential idea of 14th-century military art. The tower is 170 feet high and has four semicircular turrets at the corners. It too is surrounded by a wall and has its own moat; around the top of the wall runs a covered passage.

In the centre of the side opposite the entrance, the south side, is a tower called the **Tour du Bois,** lowered by Le Vau and transformed into a monumental entrance. In the moat on the right, at the foot of the tower called the Tour de la

Reine, is a column indicating the exact spot on which the Prince of Condé, Duke of Enghien, was executed on 20 March 1804, accused of plotting against Napoleon. The last side of the castle has five towers, all lowered in height.

Visiting the interior. The huge courtyard is entered via the **Tour du Village.** At the end on the left is the Chapel.

THE CHAPEL — Begun under Charles V in 1387, it was completed under Henri II in about 1522. In the Flamboyant Gothic style, it has stone rose windows and fine openwork on the façade. The spire has unfortunately been lost.

Interior. It is without aisles and is illuminated by large windows around the base of which runs a fine frieze. The stained glass, much restored, dates from the middle of the 16th century and depicts *Scenes from the Apocalypse.* In a chapel is the *tomb of the Duke of Enghien.*

In front of the chapel stands the **KEEP,** which since 1934 has contained a historical museum. Its three floors thus have on display relics of the kings and of great figures who lived there. The floors are all laid out in the same way: they have a vast vaulted hall with a pillar in the centre and four small rooms in the corners, originally for private use but later converted into cells. From the terrace there is a splendid view of Paris, the wood and the surrounding areas. Also in the courtyard are the two pavilions of the King and Queen. In the first, on the right, Mazarin died in 1661; the second is now occupied by the Historical Section of the Navy.

FOREST — The Bois de Vincennes, extending over 2300 acres and the largest in Paris, was given to the city by Napoleon III to be transformed into a public park. This vast area includes, in the western part, the **Lac des Minimes,** a picturesque lake with three small islands; the nearby **Indochinese Temple,** erected in memory of the Vietnamese who died in the first world war; the **Tropical Garden,** with its entrance at no. 45 Avenue de la Belle Gabrielle; and the **Floral Park,** in which hundreds of different types of flowers bloom all year round and which also contains the **exotarium,** with tropical fish and reptiles.

ZOO — Its main entrance is in Avenue Daumensil. It is one of the finest and largest zoos in Europe: it has an area of 42 acres and contains 600 mammals and 700 birds. There is also a large artificial rock 236 high, on which the mountain sheep are kept.

MUSEUM OF AFRICAN AND OCEANIAN ART — The main entrance is at no. 293 Avenue Daumensil. The building which contains the museum was constructed in 1931 for the Colonial Exhibition. The various sections of the museum include African Negro sculpture, the indigenous art of the French colonies and the economic and social life of the African countries.

Bois de Boulogne - La Villette - La Défense

BOIS DE BOULOGNE

Situated to the west of Paris, almost opposite the other park of Vincennes, the Bois de Boulogne, with its lawns, lakes, waterfalls and gardens, covers an area of more than 2200 acres. In the era of the Merovingian kings, it was a vast forest, called the Forêt du Rouvre, from the name of an oak-tree which grew abundantly there. In the 16th century, a church called Notre-Dame-de-Boulogne-sur-mer was erected, and gradually the name of Boulogne came to replace that of Rouvre. The place became a refuge for adventurers and bandits, so that in 1556 Henri II had it surrounded by a high wall with eight gates. It was replanned by Colbert and Louis XIV opened its gates to the public, with the result that the wood became a favourite place for promenades. Devastated in 1815 by the English and Russian armies when they camped there, the wood was given to the city in 1852 by Napoleon III, who commissioned Haussmann to replan and reorganise it: thus the wood became a vast park, inspired by London's Hyde Park, which the emperor had admired. Today the Bois de Boulogne includes lakes (the **Lac Supérieur** and **Lac Inférieur**), waterfalls (the **Grande-Cascade**), parks (a splendid one is that of the **Bagatelle,** with the two mansions of the **Château** and **Trianon**), museums (the **Museum of Popular Arts and Traditions**) and famous sporting centres (the **Longchamps Racecourse,** where the Gran Prix is run every year, and the **Auteuil Racecourse**).

THE VILLETTE

A market for livestock as far back as 1867, in 1979 the park of the Villette (35 hectares) was predisposed as the site of the largest museum ever dedicated to science and technology. Structures include the «Géode» (a vast hemispherical projection hall), the «Grande Halle» (one of the finest metal buildings of the 19th century), and the «Zénith», a hall for entertainments.

The large Geode.

The Great Arch built in the Défense district.

THE «GRANDE ARCHE»

Designed in 1982 by the Dane Johan Otto von Spreckelsen and inaugurated in July, 1989, the Grande Arche consists of two towers 105 meters high topped by a crosspiece. At the center of the structure faced in Carrara marble and glass hangs a sort of large awning, the so-called «Cloud». Four elevators carry visitors to the evocative belvedere.

LA DEFENSE

Urbanism of la Défense, conceived as a huge 130 hectare business area, commenced in 1955 in the area forming the extension of Neuilly bridge. Buildings are erected below a paved esplanade 120 metres long and 250 metres wide, with steps down to the Seine and under which all highways pass. Of all the modern buildings characterized by pure, geometric shapes (Fiat, Manhattan, Gian, Elf-Aquitaine towers), the number one attraction is the C.N.I.T. building, where fairs are held every year. Built in coats of concrete by the architects Zehrfuss, Camelot and Mailly, it has the audacious shape of an overturned shell resting on only three points of support.

Entrance courtyard of the palace with statue of Louis XIV.

VERSAILLES

HISTORY – Situated about 14 miles south-west of Paris, Versailles at the time of Louis XIII was no more than a modest hunting lodge, built in 1624 and consisting of a simple square building with the present-day Marble Court in the centre. The creation of the great palace of Versailles was due to Louis XIV, who after the Fronda incidents decided to abandon Paris and transform his predecessor's simple hunting castle into a royal palace worthy of the splendid sovereign he wished to be. In 1668 Le Vau enlarged the original building to twice its size, giving it a wide façade on the side overlooking the park. The work of transforming the palace continued for a long time, under the direction of the other architects Hardouin-Mansart and Le Nôtre. The latter concentrated mainly on laying out the great gardens. On 6 October 1789, the royal family returned finally from Versailles to Paris in their gilded carriage, after a procession of market women had marched on the palace in an unprecedented demonstration. Without the royal court, the castle fell into a state of nearly

The entrance to the Royal Palace of Versailles.

Parterres of water in front of the Royal Palace.

total abandon, being sacked many times and robbed of many of its works of art, until in 1837 Louis-Philippe restored it and converted it into a museum of French history. Occupied by the Germans in 1870, it was the scene of the coronation of William of Prussia as emperor of Germany. In 1875 the Republic of France was proclaimed and in 1919 the peace treaty with Germany, putting an end to the first world war, was signed there.

PALACE — Entering through the main gateway (which under Louis XIV was opened every morning at 5.30), we reach the first courtyard, called the **Ministers' Court,** at the end of which is the statue on horseback of Louis XIV (1835, by Cartellier and Petitot), with the two long buildings called the **Ministers' Wings** at the sides. Access to the second courtyard, the **Royal Court,** was permitted only to the carriages of the royal family: this has the **Gabriel Wing** or **Wing of Louis XV** on the right and the **Old Wing** on the left. Finally, there is the third courtyard, the **Marble Court,** surrounded by the original building, the castle of Louis XIII, with its red bricks alternating with white stone. The three windows behind the balcony in the centre belonged to the king's bedroom: it was from here that, on 1 September 1715, at 8,15 in the morning, the death of Louis XIV was announced; on the same balcony, 74 years later, Louis XVI appeared to placate the people who wanted him to return to Paris.

Through an arcade in the Royal Court, the **western façade** of the palace, the most famous and most splendid façade, is reached. More than 1700 feet long, it overlooks the pleasant gardens. The central, projecting part was designed by Le Vau, while Hardouin-Mansart designed its two elegant wings. Each part consists of two orders, the lower of rusticated arcades and the upper of pillars, with pilaster strips and high windows. Above these again is a balustraded attic, in which were the apartments of the various members of the huge court, whereas the central part and two wings were where the family of the king and the royal princes lived.

Interior. The interior is reached from the Royal Court by way of the Gabriel Wing. After the two vestibules comes the **Historical Museum,** with its eleven rooms illustrating the eras of Louis XIII and Louis XIV. At the end of the first gallery, via a stairway, is the entrance to the **Opéra,** designed by Gabriel in 1770 for the marriage of Louis XVI and Marie-Antoinette: it is an oval-shaped chamber, with fine wood inlays and gilding on a blue background. Moving up to the first floor, particular attention should be given to the **Chapel,** built to a design by Hardouin-Mansart between 1698 and 1710. It has three aisles, square pillars on which the arcades rest, and above them a gallery with fluted columns.

From the Chapel, we reach the **Hercules Saloon,** vestibule of the **Great Apartment of the King,** consisting of six Saloons richly decorated with stuccoes, polychrome marble

A foreshortened image of the Gallery of Battles and a general view of the King's bedroom.

The Hall of Mirrors.

and tapestries. Here the sovereign received the court three times a week, from six until ten o'clock in the evening. The saloons take their names from the various mythological subjects painted in the frescoes on the ceilings: thus the **Abundance Saloon** is followed by the **Venus Saloon**; the **Saloon of Diana** (with a *bust* by Bernini depicting Louis XIV), which was the billiard room; the **Mars Saloon**, used as a ballroom, with a magnificent Gobelins tapestry

representing the *entrance of Louis XIV into Dunkirk;* the **Mercury Saloon,** once a games room, where the body of Louis XIV lay in state for eight days; the **Apollo Saloon,** the music room, though during the day it became the throne room. Through the **War Saloon,** with its cupola painted by Le Brun and with a fine stucco medallion by Coysevox depicting *Louis XIV on horseback,* we reach the celebrated **Hall of Mirrors.** A masterpiece designed by Hardouin-Mansart and built between 1678 and 1684, it is 246 feet long and 33 feet wide and its ceiling is decorated with paintings by Le Brun illustrating French victories. Seventeen large windows look out onto the park, corresponding to the same number of windows on the wall opposite; at the time of Louis XIV, the hall was illuminated in the evening by the light of 3000 candles. It was also embellished with tapestries, statues and orange trees in silver vases. At the end of the Hall of Mirrors is the **Peace Saloon,** so called because of the oval painting over the fireplace depicting *Louis XV bringing Peace to Europe* (Lemoyne, 1729).

Next to the Hall is the **Suite of the King.** This consists of the **Council Chamber,** where Louis XIV used to work with his ministers; the **King's Bedchamber,** decorated with white and gold wood, where Louis XIV died; and the famous **Bull's Eye Saloon,** in which the court dignitaries every morning and evening were present when the king rose and went to bed. Splendid too is the **Private Suite of the King,** in the Louis XV style. Returning to the Peace Saloon, we pass on to the **Suite of the Queen,** built between 1671 and 1680. It consists of the **Queen's Bedchamber;** the **Saloon of the Nobles,** with the original furniture which was there in 1789; an **Antechamber,** with magnificent *Gobelins tapestries* and a *portrait of Marie-Antoinette,* by Vigée-Lebrun; the **Queen's Guards' Room,** where on 6 October 1789 a group of insurgents from Paris killed several guards who were defending Marie-Antoinette. From this room one can visit the six small rooms in pure Louis XVI style which make up the so-called **Private Suite of the Queen.** Then, by the **Queen's Staircase,** designed by Hardouin-Mansart, we reach the **Great Guardroom,** in which there are two works by David, representing the *Coronation of Napoleon* and the *Distribution of the Eagles,* and one by Gros, representing *Murat at the Battle of Aboukir.* Nearby is the splendid **Battle Gallery,** built by Louis-Philippe in 1836: it takes its name from the paintings illustrating the most famous battles in France's history, among them the Battle of Taillebourg, painted by Delacroix. Again by way of the Queen's Stairway, we go on to the rooms on the ground floor, decorated in Louis XIV style, with paintings from the reigns of Louis XV and Louis XVI.

GARDENS — These are considered the prototype of the French-style garden because of their elegant style, full of artistic and scenographic inventions. The gardens were designed by Le Nôtre between 1661 and 1668 and occupy an area of nearly 250 acres. The best panoramic view is without doubt from the terrace: at its ends are the two fountains, the **fountain of Diana** on the right and the **Point-du-Jour fountain** on the left, surrounded by bronze statues. On one side of the terrace are the **northern flower beds**

The Basin of Apollo.

with basins and statues, among them the Venus with the Tortoise, by Coysevox, a copy of the classical **Knife-grinder**, and the so-called **Fountain of the Pyramid,** by Girardon. Nearby the **basin of the Nymphs of Diana** and the **Allée des Marmousets,** a double row of 22 basins adorned with bronze putti from which the fountains spurt: this takes us as far as the **Basin of the Dragons** and the **Basin of Neptune** (1740).

On the south side of the terrace are the box-edged **southern flower beds.** From the balcony can be seen the **Orangerie,** which contains 3000 trees (oranges, almonds and pomegranates). Each year more than 150,000 types of flowers were planted there. Nearby are the great **Stairways of 100 Steps** and the **Swiss Lake,** made between 1678 and 1682 by the Swiss Guards: at the end of it is a statue by Bernini representing Louis XIV, which Girardon transformed into the statue of Marcus Curtius.

From the central terrace, we descend to the **Basin of Latona,** a masterpiece by Marsy depicting the goddess with her children Diana and Apollo, dominating the concentric basins which ascend in the form of a pyramid. This fountain stands at the beginning of the long avenue called the **Tapis-Vert** (Green Carpet), at the other end of which is the great **Basin of Apollo.** In it Tuby depicted the god's chariot drawn by four horses emerging triumphant from the water to illuminate the sky, while the tritons blow into their shells to announce Apollo's arrival. Behind this sculptural group a vast area of green stretches out, interrupted by the **Grand Canal** (more than 200 feet wide and more than a mile long), which is in turn met halfway along by the **Small Canal**. There are groves, pools and fountains all around: the **Dôme Grove,** by Hardouin-Mansart, the **Obelisk Grove,** by the same designer, the grove of the **Apollo Baths,** the **Basin of the Putti,** adorned with sculpture done by Hardy in 1710, and the **Enceladus Basin,** with the statue by Marsy depicting the giant who was crushed under a mountain of rocks.

THE TRIANONS — This is another impressive example of the luxury and the sumptuous life which the court led at Versailles.

THE GRAND TRIANON — This building was erected in a corner of the park of Versailles for Louis XIV, who used to say that the Trianon had been made for him, whereas Versailles was for the court. It was built by Mansart in 1687 in the classical forms of an Italian palazzo: with a single storey and large windows with Doric pilasters between them, the whole structure made from delicate pink marble. Against the architect's advice, Louis XIV also ordered the construction of the peristyle with columns and pillars which unites the two wings to the rest of the building.

Interior. The part of the building on the right includes the **reception apartments,** as well as the **apartment of Napoleon I** (in which the royal mistresses Mme de Maintenon and Mme de Pompadour had lived previously) and the **apartment of Louis XIV,** occupied by the king from 1703 up to his death. In the left-hand part is the **apartment of Monseigneur,** who was the son of Louis XIV, with fine Louis XIV wood panelling.

THE PETIT TRIANON — Built by Gabriel for Louis XV in 1762, it is considered the palace of the royal mistresses of France. Madame de Pompadour died there in 1764 and it then became the king's favourite place for spending his free time with the Countess du Barry. Louis XVI made a symbolic gift of it to Marie-Antoinette and Napoleon gave it to his sister Pauline. With its simple façade and graceful columns, elegant style and fine proportions, the building can be considered the first example of the Neoclassical style. Inside it retains the furniture which belonged to Marie-Antoinette.

In the garden arounds the Trianons, it is worth paying a visit to the small **Temple of Love,** built in 1778 by Mique, with twelve Corinthian columns and a cupola, beneath which is the statue of an adolescent Cupid, and the **Queen's Hamlet,** a picturesque imitation rustic village, with thatched cottages, a dairy and a mill, once driven by the waters of a small stream. Designed by the painter Hubert Robert between 1783 and 1786, this was Marie-Antoinette's favourite place, where she often came to spend time in the open air, pretending to be a simple country lady.

INDEX

© Copyright 1994 by Casa Editrice Bonechi
Via Cairoli 18/b - 50131 Firenze - Italia
Tel. 055/576841 - Telex 571323 CEB - Fax 055/5000766

Diffusion:
OVET 13, rue des Nanettes - 75011 Paris
Tel. (1) 43.385.750

Printed in Italy by Centro Stampa Editoriale Bonechi.

PHOTOGRAPH REFERENCES
Photographs from the Archives of the Casa Editrice Bonechi by:

G.Boullay: page 23.

G. Dagli Orti: pages 26;27;81;91;97;98;105;106;109;110;148;
149 bottom;151;152-153;155.

U. Falugi: pages 28;66;78;92;113;133;135;137;138;145.

V. Gauvreau: pages 70;89;93;147.

P. Giambone :pages 4;11;12;14;15;16;17;18;19;20;21;22;25;30;31;33;
34;35;36;37;61;62;65;68;72;73;74;77 bottom;79;80;95;99;100;101;
104;108;115;117;120;121;122;123;124;125;126;140;141;142;146.

Museés Nationaux: pages 40;41;43;47;48;50;51;53;54;55;56;58;
59;62;75;76.

J. C. Pinheira: pages 2;60;63;69;136;139;149 top.

A. Pistolesi: pages 77 top;82;83;84;85;86;87.

The publisher wishes to thank the Grand Louvre Press Office for having kindly authorised the reproduction of the plans on page 39.

ISBN 88-8029-134-3